ROYDEN RABINOWITCH

—To the memory of Max Wandeler

Max was a truly wonderfully beautiful person who was utterly fascinated by my approach to things and events. Both of us were, early in our lives, deeply disturbed by the simple fact that any real physical understanding was a function of accepting the severance of feeling from things and events. And Max was surprised and delighted that he had met somebody who had devoted his whole life to addressing this disturbance while he, as he told me, devoted his whole life to running away from this disturbance. He always thought that I was courageous and I could never convince him that I lacked the strength and spirit to run away, caught as I was, in the headlights of this disturbance. That Max is no longer here and will never see this monograph breaks my heart.

—Royden Rabinowitch

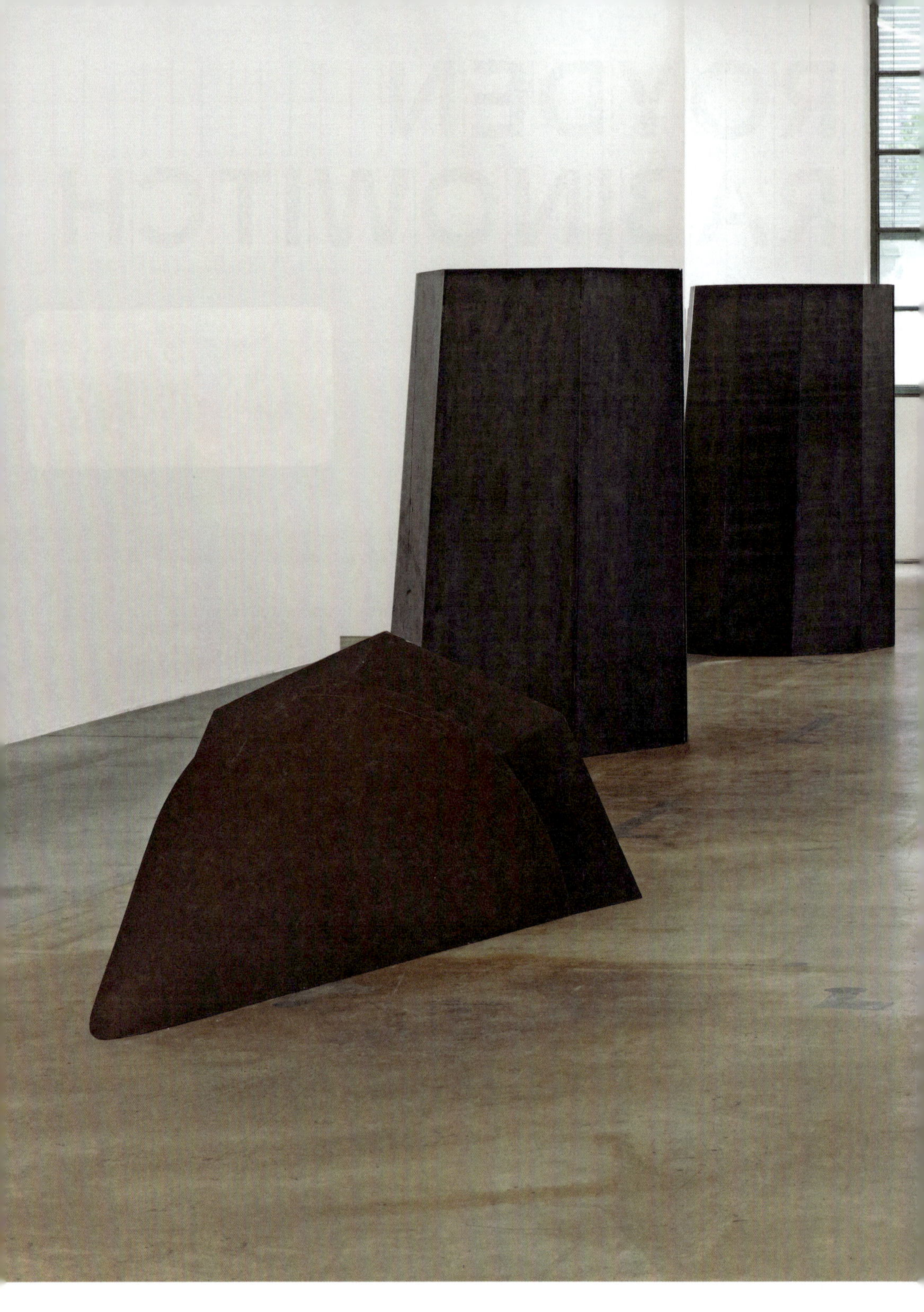

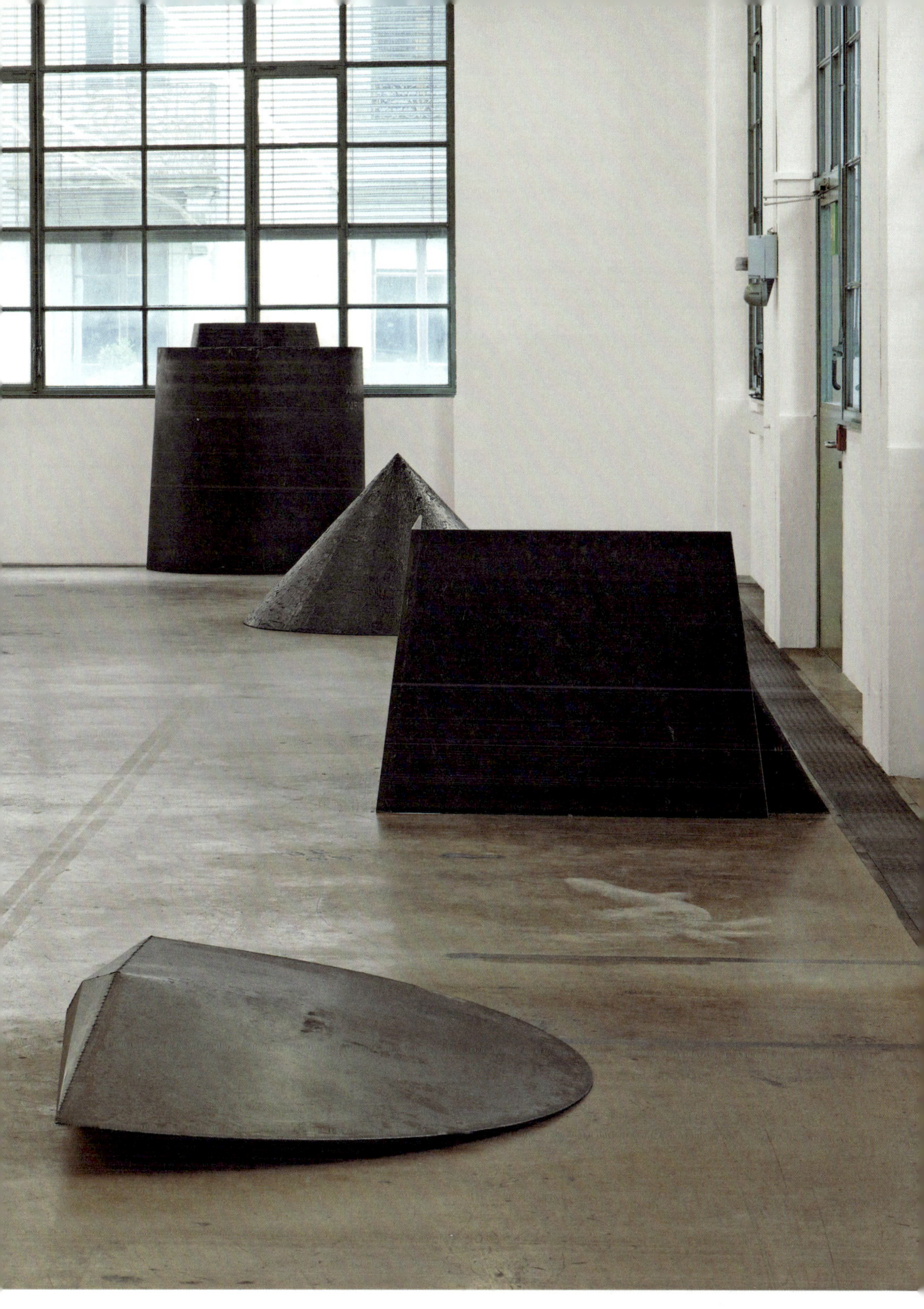

L'Éternel Détour/2, MAMCO, 2011

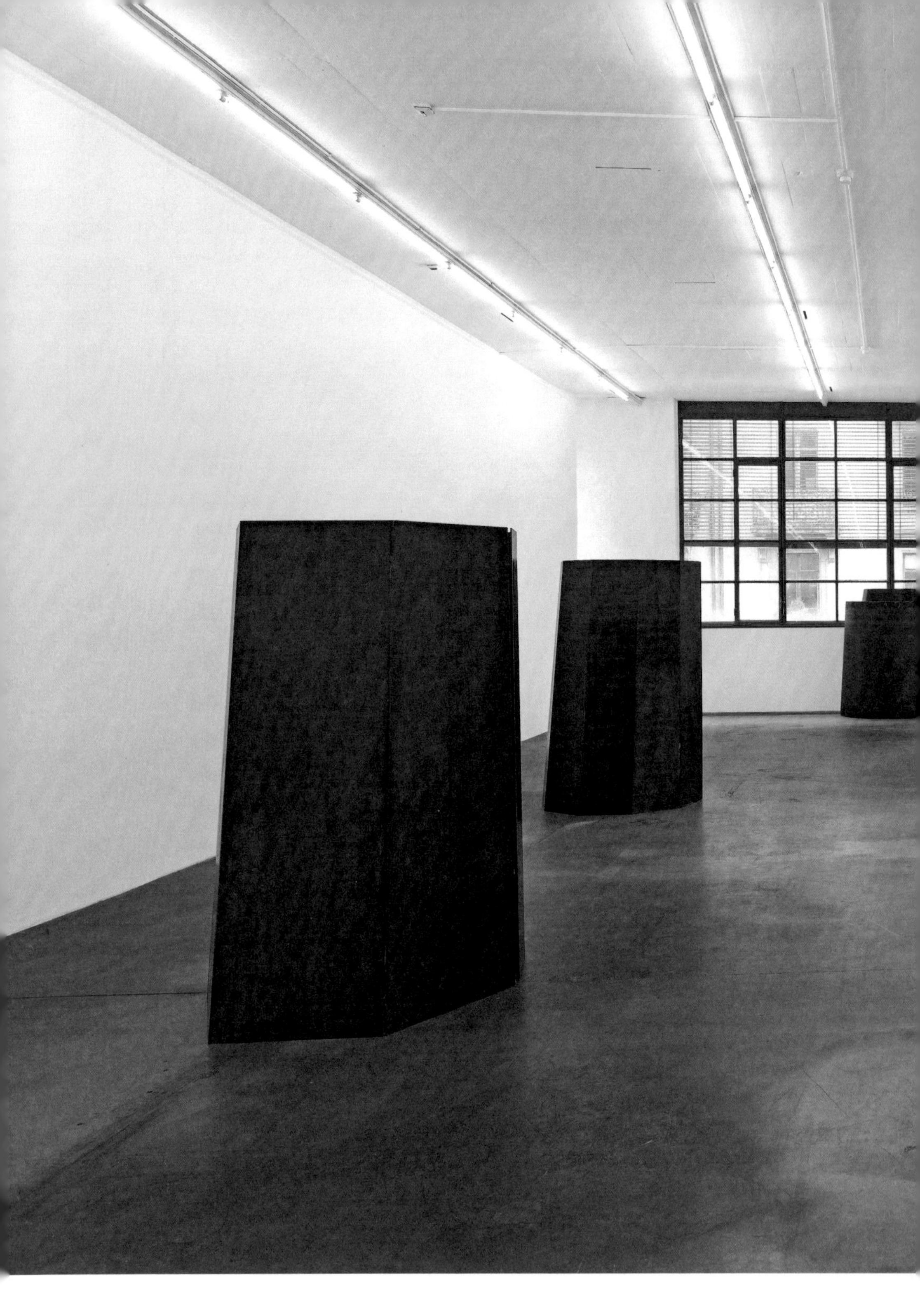

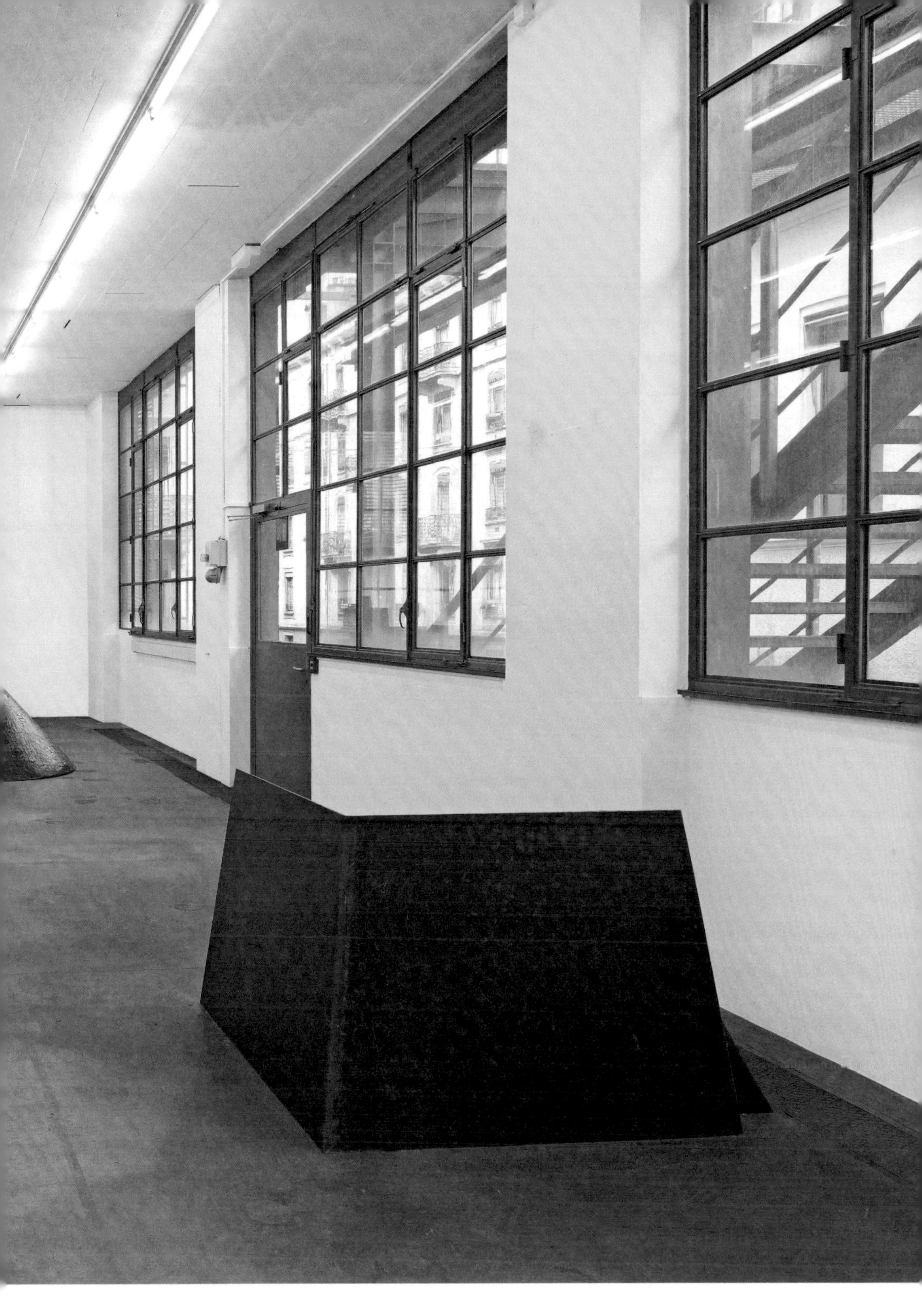

L'Éternel Détour/2, MAMCO, 2011

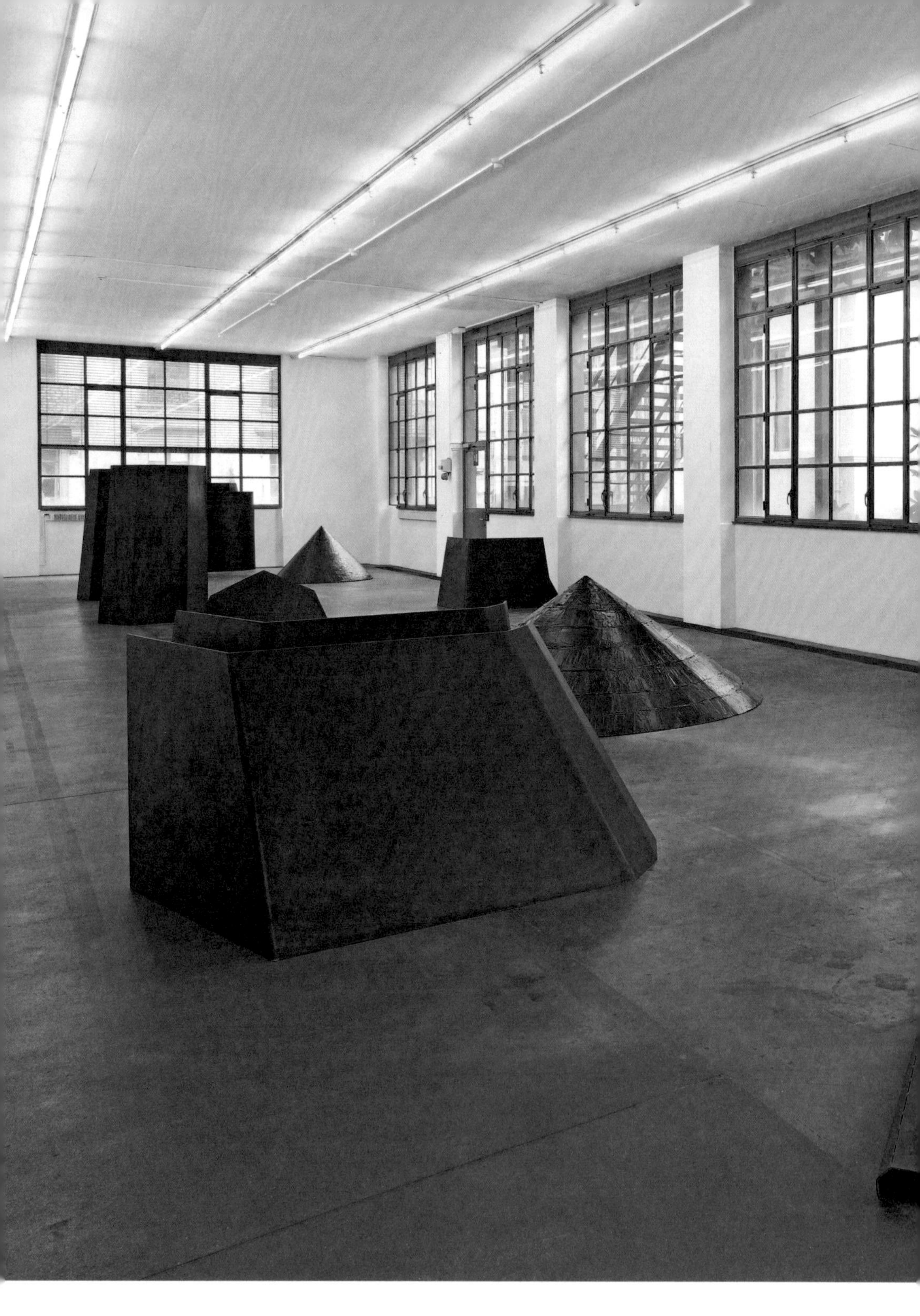

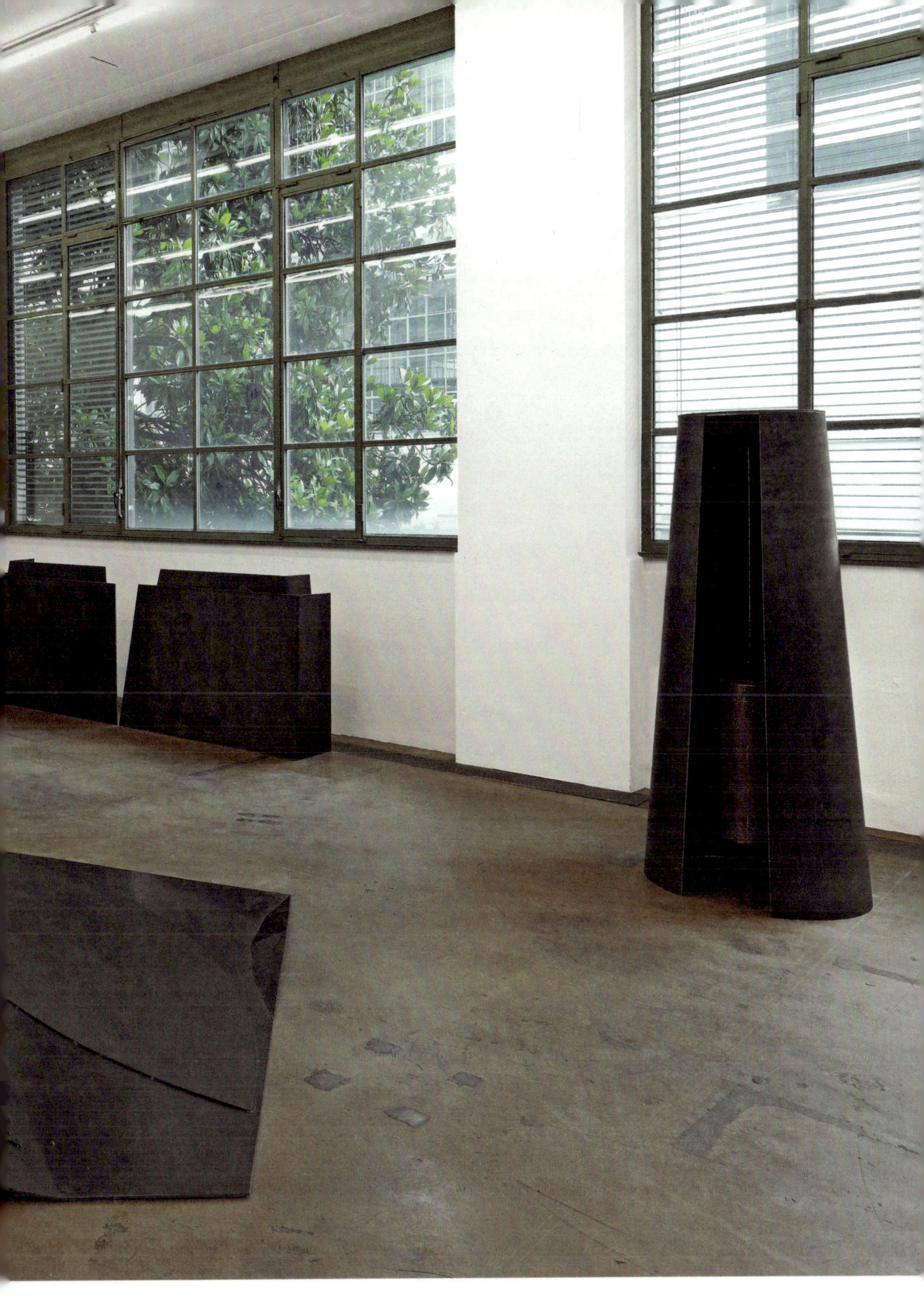

L'Éternel Détour/2, MAMCO, 2011

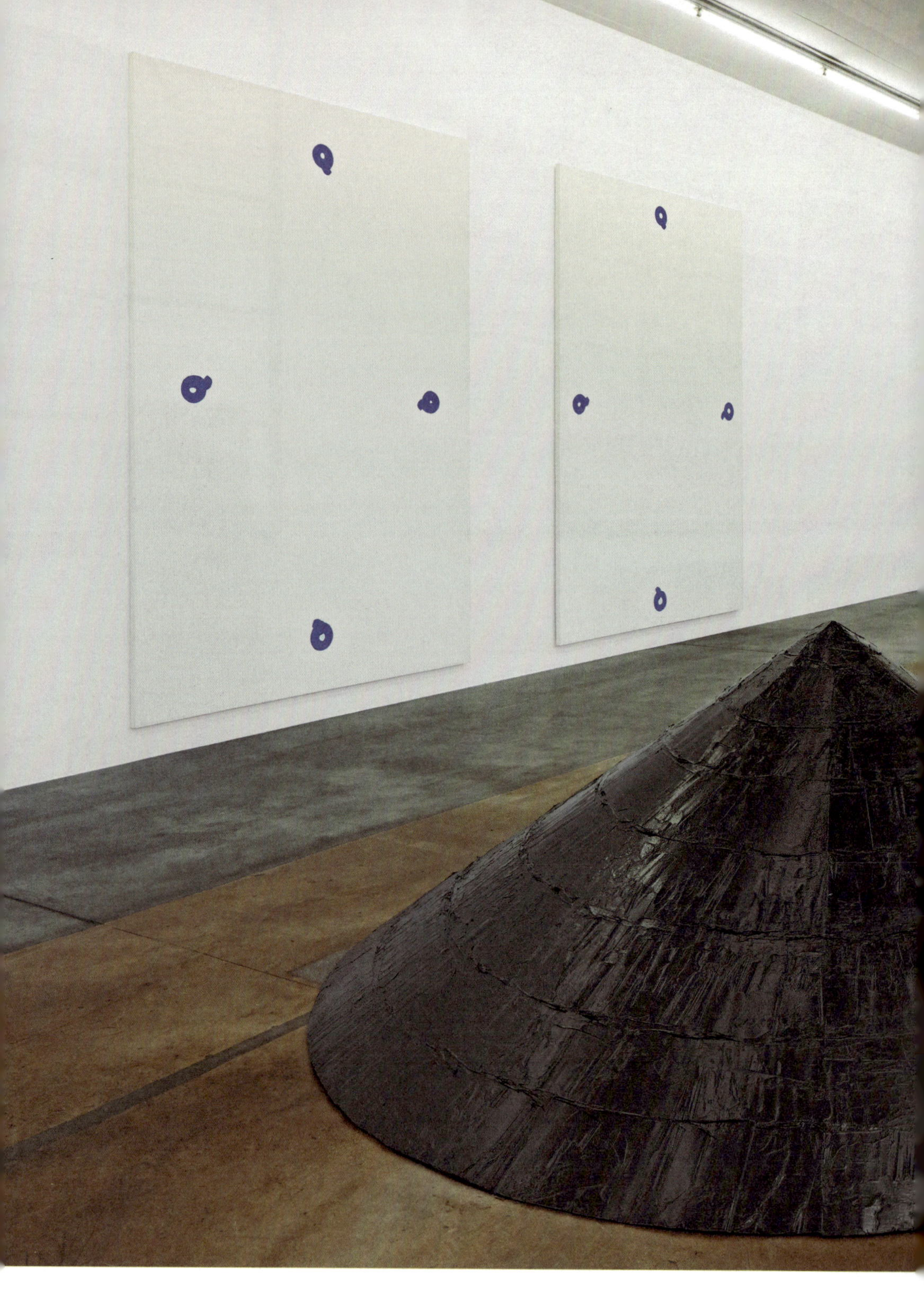

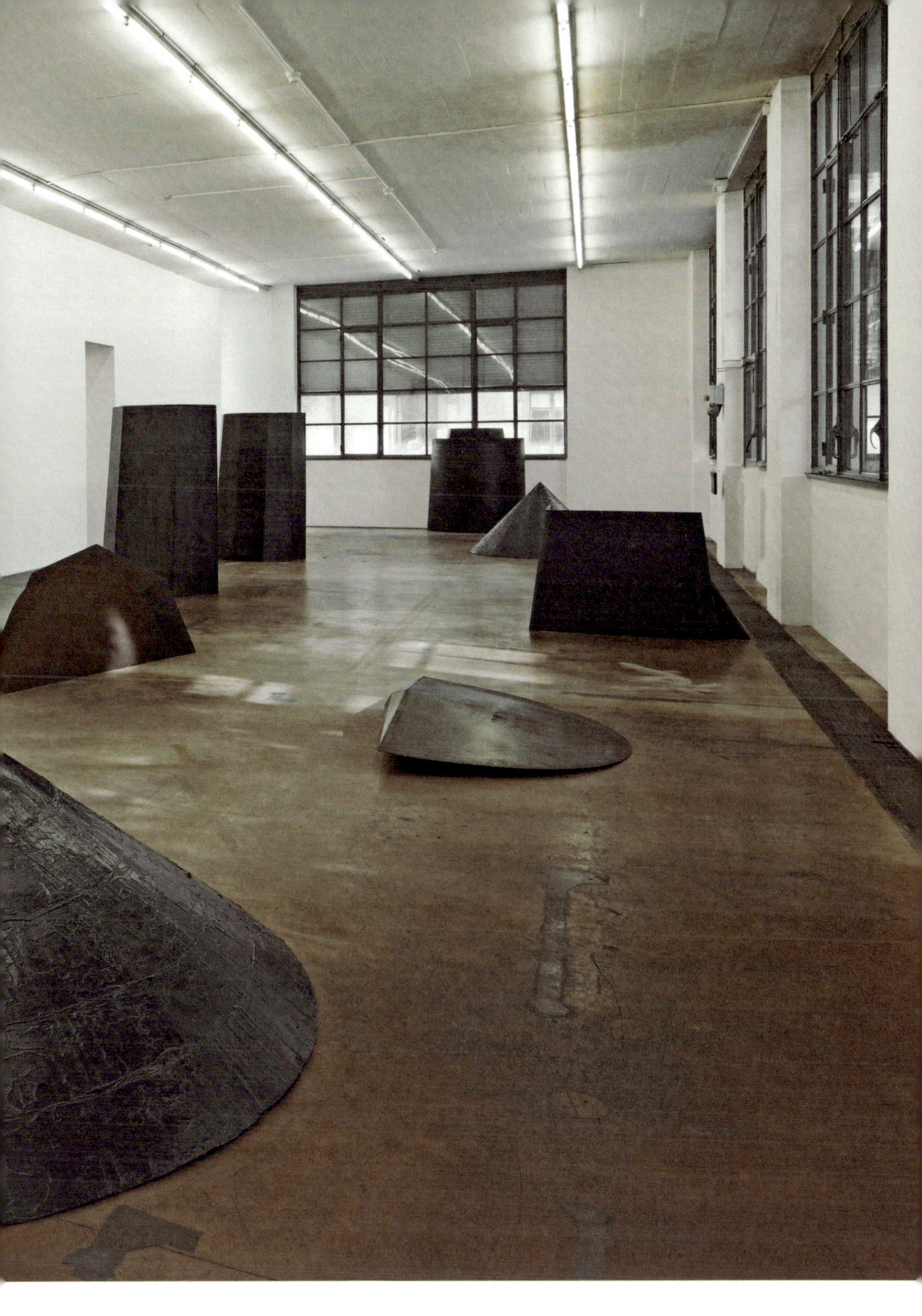

L'Éternel Détour/2, MAMCO, 2011

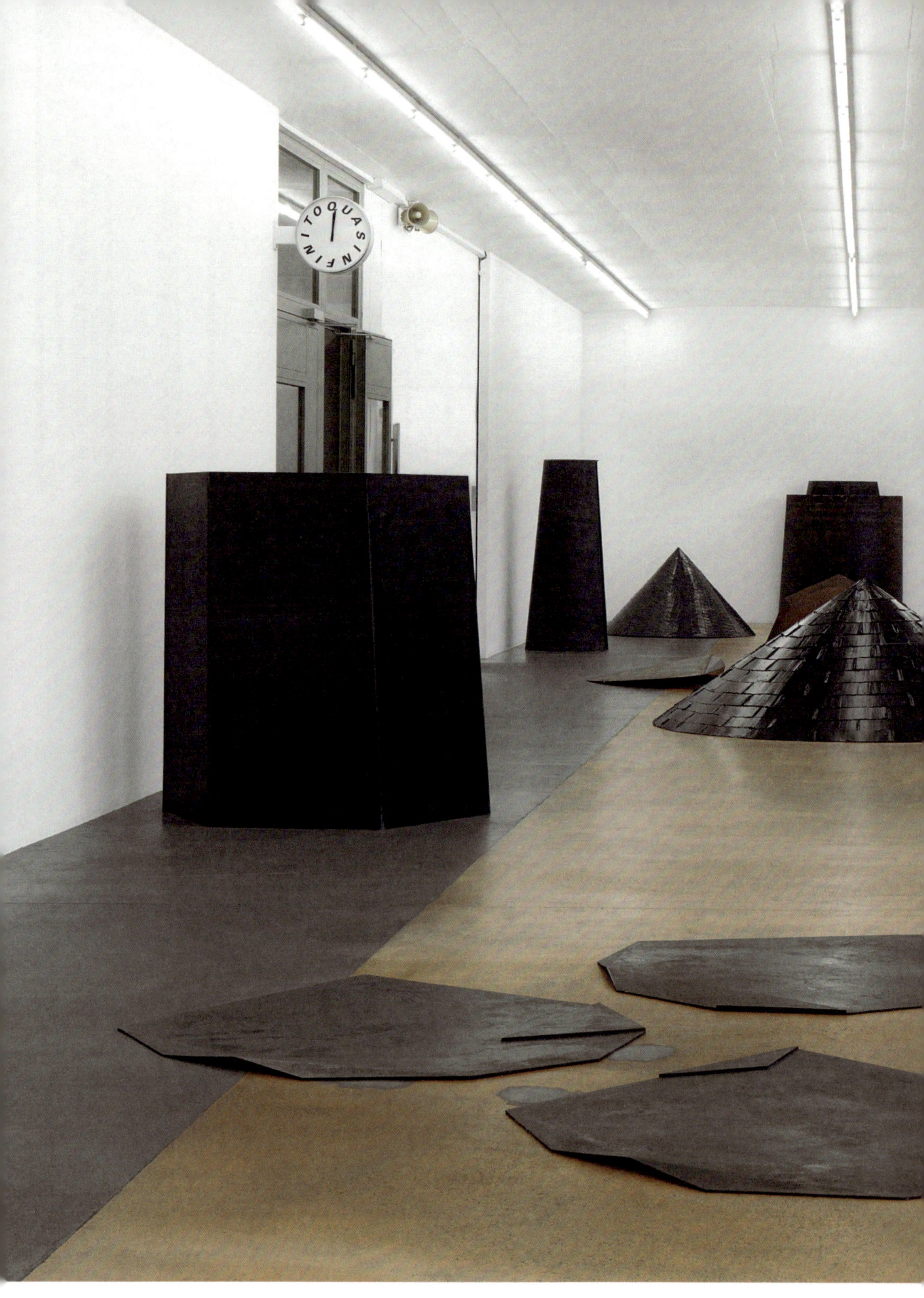
QUASINFINITO

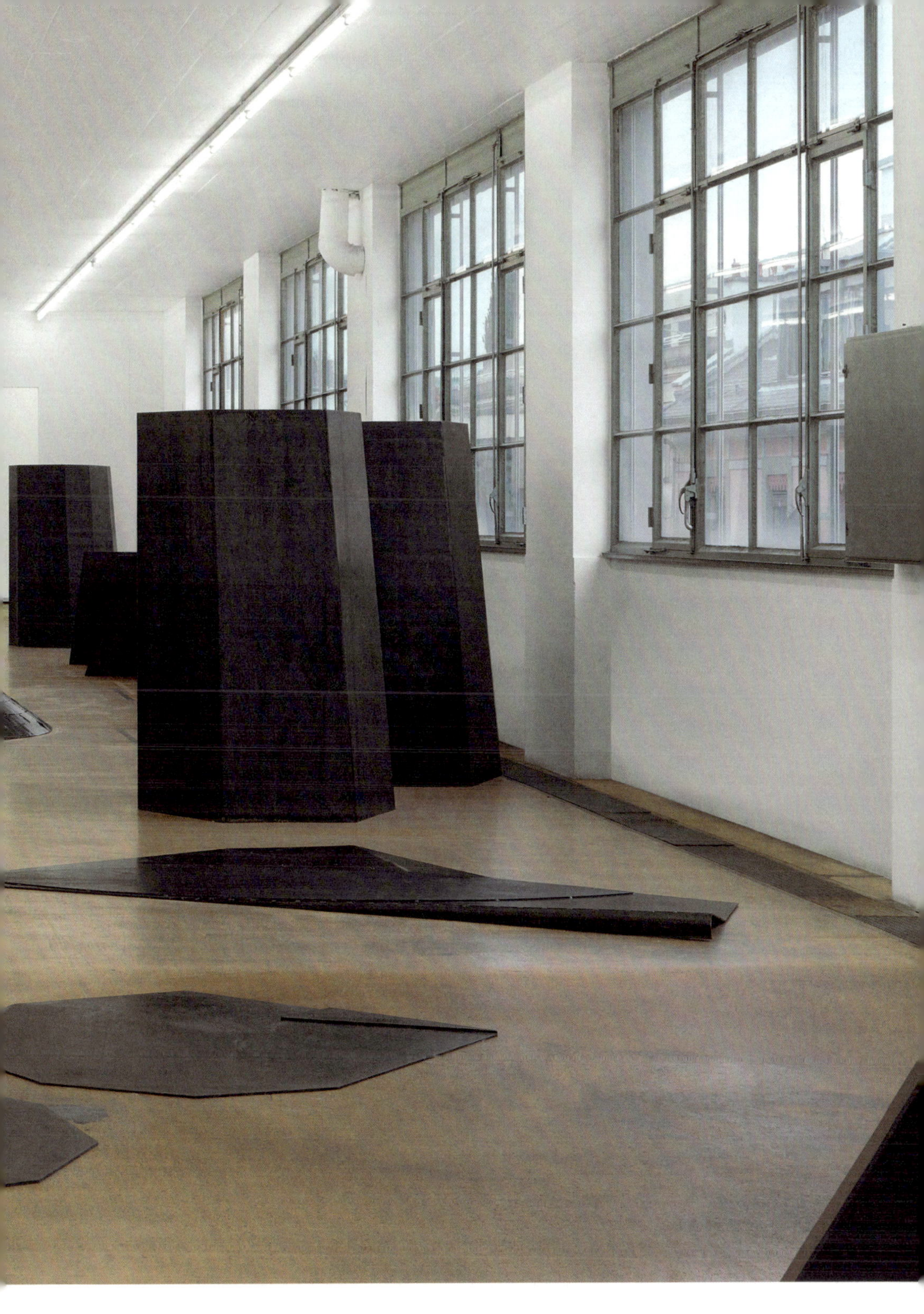

Récit d'un temps court, MAMCO, 2017

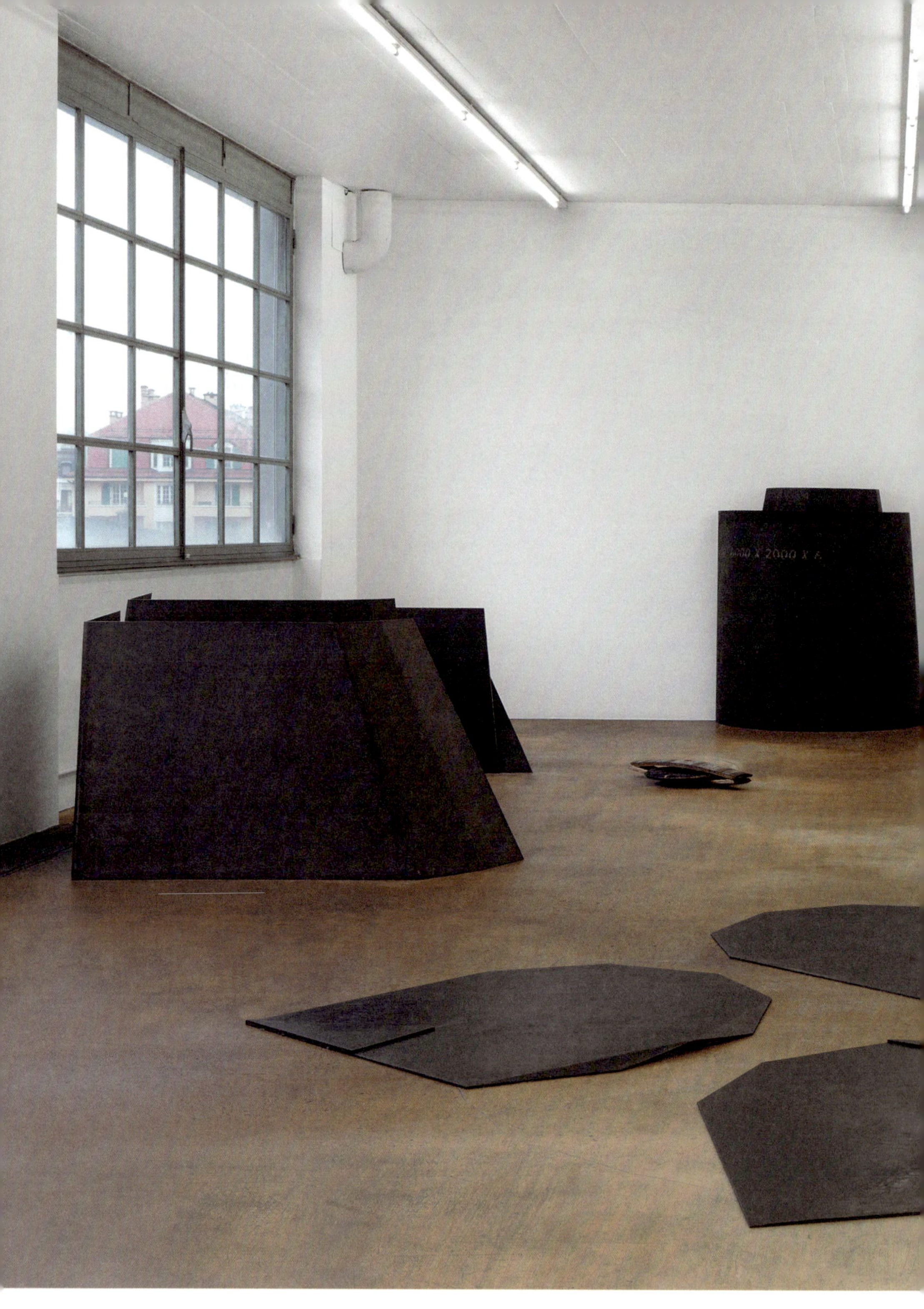

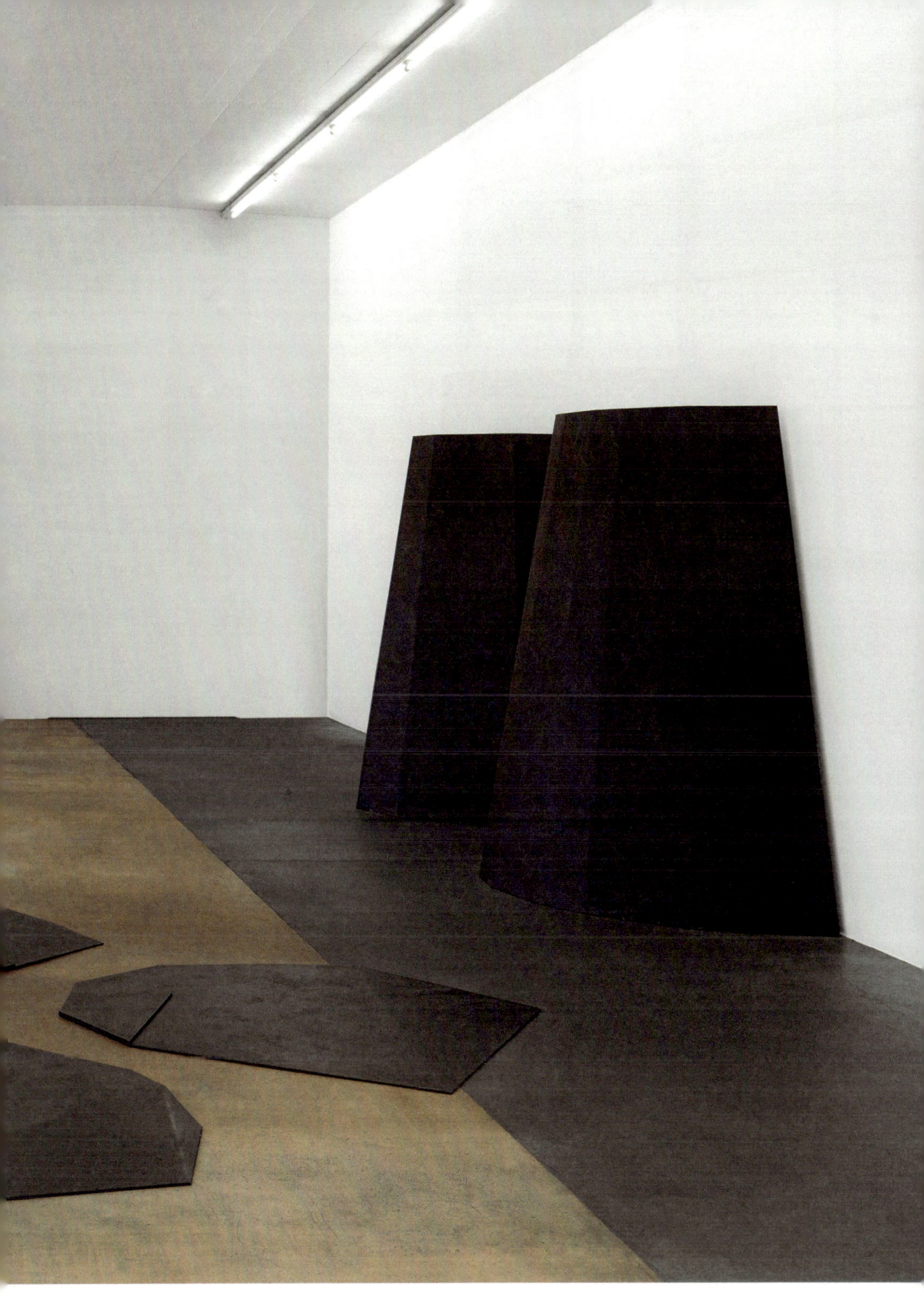

Récit d'un temps court, MAMCO, 2017

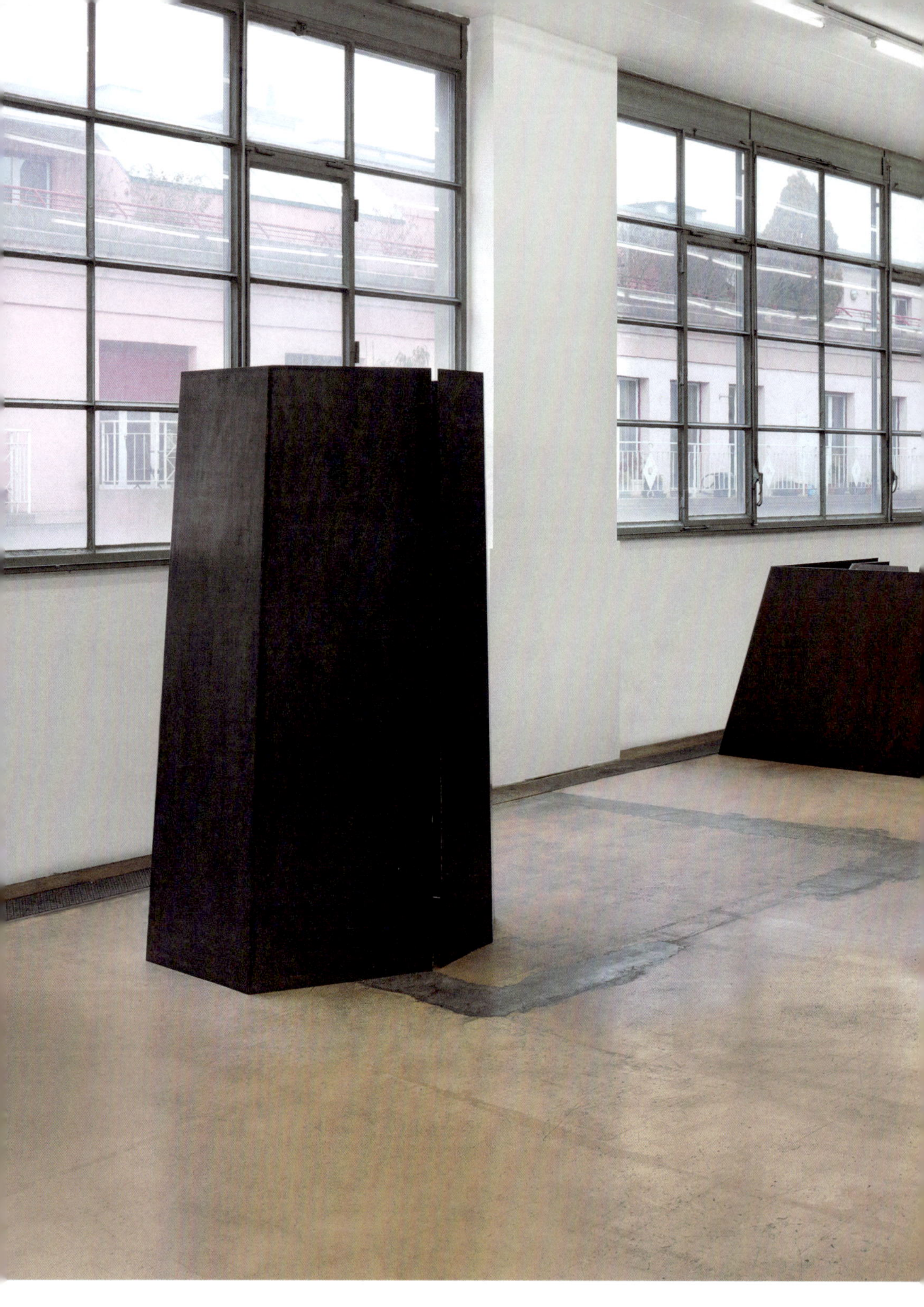

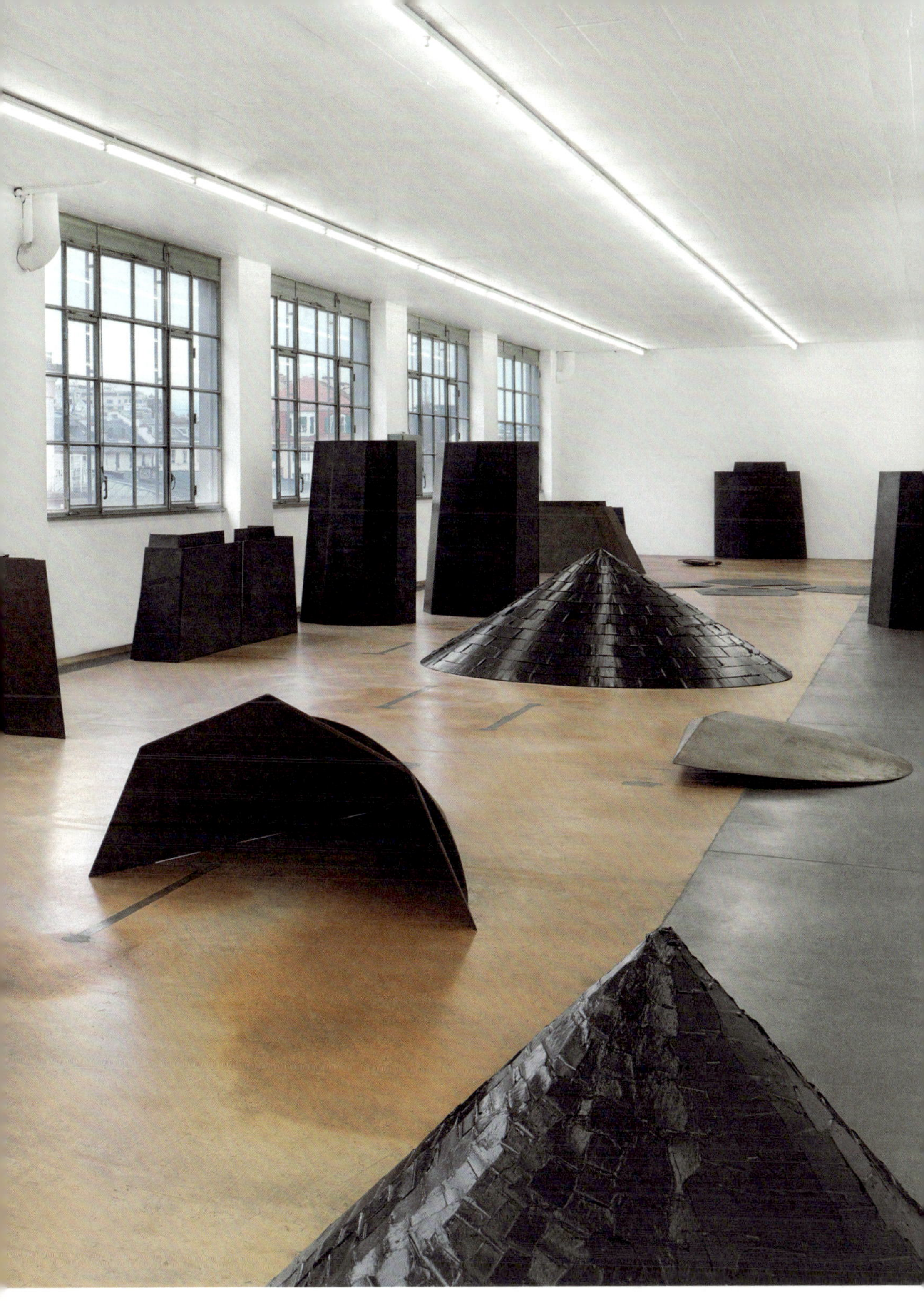

Récit d'un temps court, MAMCO, 2017

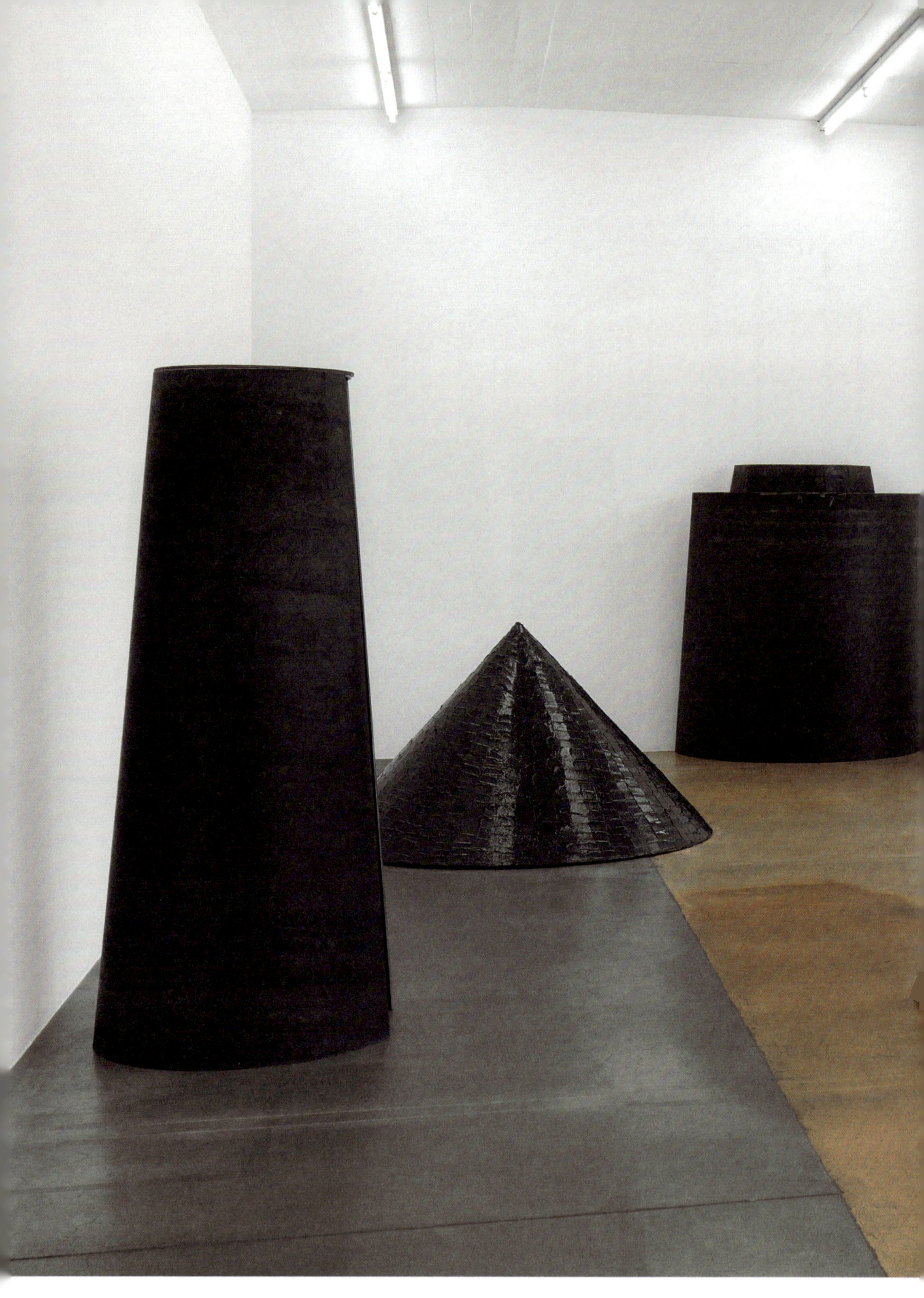

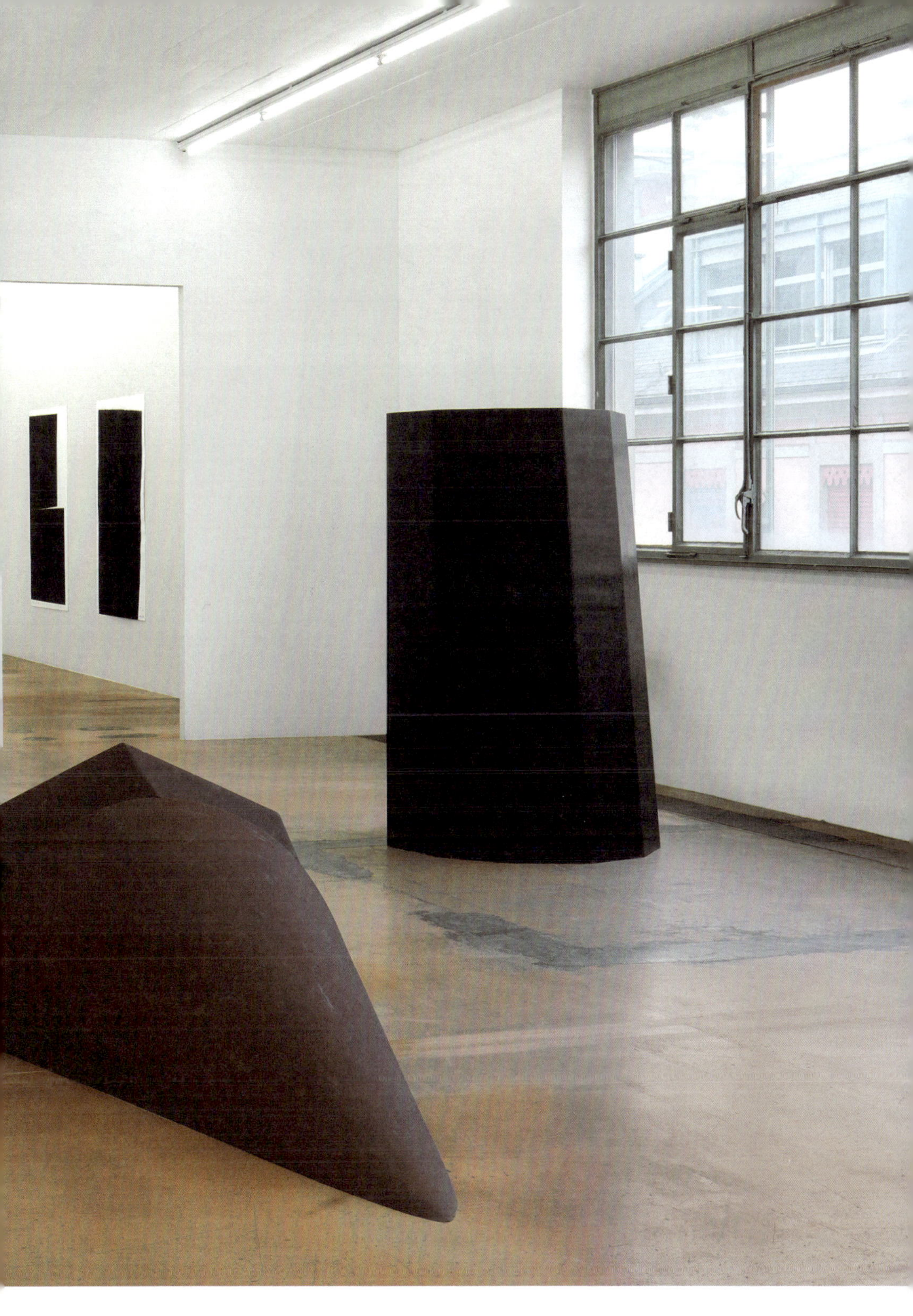

Récit d'un temps court, MAMCO, 2017

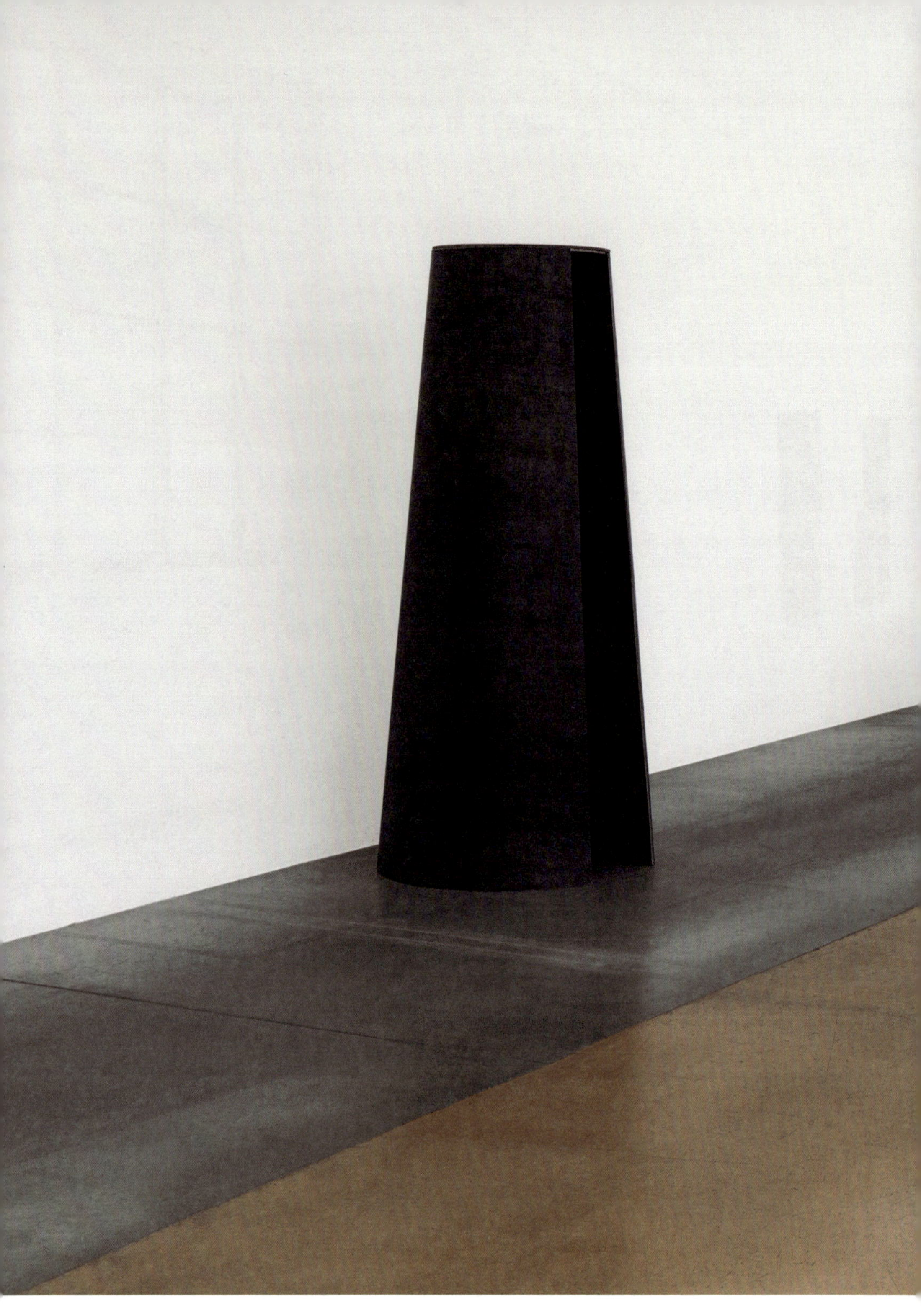

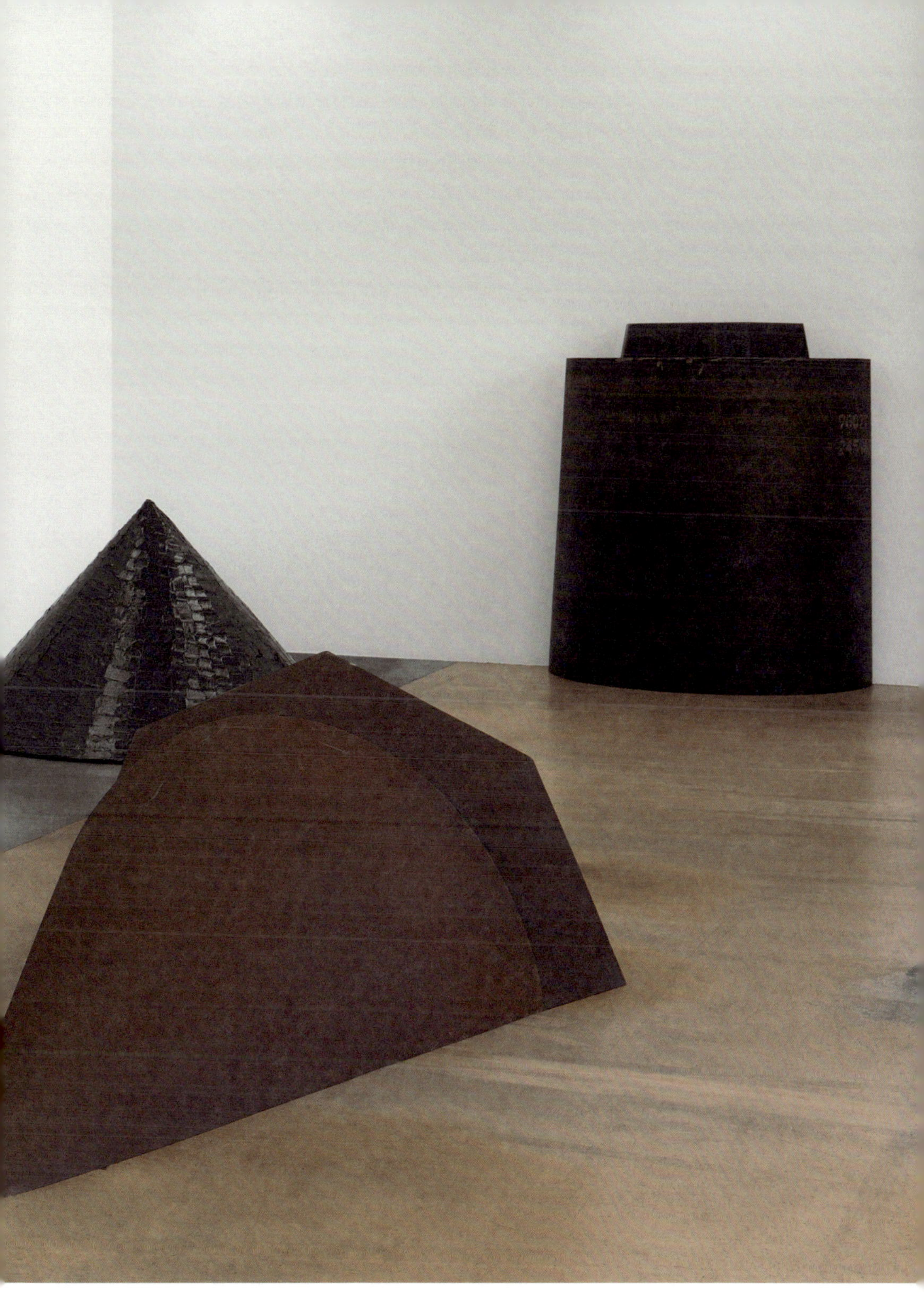

Récit d'un temps court, MAMCO, 2017

TABLE OF CONTENTS

22

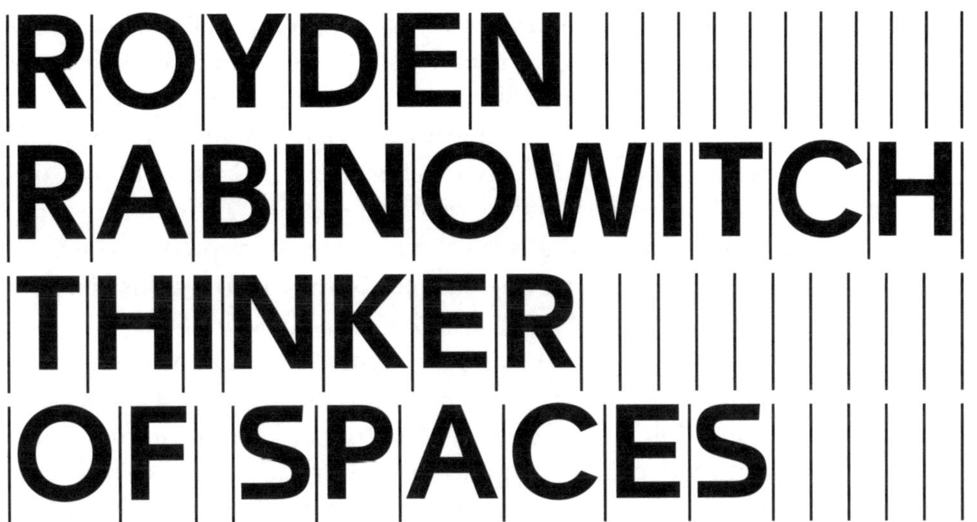

Alessandro Gallicchio

Royden Rabinowitch's work is a complex constellation of sculptures and drawings, arising out of his profound reflections on the forces governing volumes, spaces, and the bodily experience of the observer. He has always laid claim to multiple interests, ranging from the history of science to the history of art, and including also natural history and the history of architecture, and he has always taken an almost scientific approach to art and its objects, handling with ease concepts from the fields of mathematics, cognitive science, and physics. This familiarity with science and its methods has given him the means to create forms that combine convex and concave pieces, open and closed spaces, flat and folded surfaces, continuous and discontinuous lines, always with the aim of questioning the relations between observers and objects. It is within this universe of constructive rigour that we must situate the rich production of this artist, who began his artistic career in Toronto, Canada, far from the main centers of international sculpture. Indeed, it was in Toronto, between 1962 and 1965, that Rabinowitch was to lay the foundation of his work, before moving to New York City in 1975, where he was to further develop his sculptural language through fruitful encounters with the Minimalists and European Modernists of that city.

Art, Science, and Music: The Formative Years

Royden Rabinowitch attaches great importance to his formative period, and there can be no doubt that this period has had a determining influence on the development of his thinking. His artistic training took place in the aftermath of debates born out of abstraction and its various interpretations in the post-war period. Taking his place within this context, although all the while refusing to participate actively in it, Rabinowitch was a contributor to what Rudi Fuchs has called the fifth generation of abstract artists.[1] Indeed, it was precisely through his contact with the work of such a master of contemporary sculpture as

David Smith that Rabinowitch claims to have first discovered, at the age of 14 years, the significance of the spatial relations produced by assemblages of volumes of steel. After visiting Smith's retrospective exhibition, in 1957 at the Museum of Modern Art in New York, Rabinowitch was to go, from time to time, to Smith's studio, considered at the time the most visible locus of anthropomorphic sculpture. Smith worked on the basis of open pieces that made explicit reference to pictorial abstraction. In 1956, he created a major work, *Five Units Equal*, that Rabinowitch saw as a geometrical construction incorporating a grouping of spatial possibilities that could not be reconciled into a whole.[2] It was this sculpture, at this particular time, that Rabinowitch says revealed to him the essential confusion that exists between the notions of geometrical space and concrete space, the former referring to abstract space, i.e. a continuous and infinite geometrical projection, and the latter indicating the ordinary space of experience, i.e. the discontinuous and finite conditions of perception. Smith's artwork was essentially the translation into sculpture of Henri Poincaré's distinction, made at the beginning of the century, between abstract space and the space of experience—a distinction that Rabinowitch had discovered through his long conversations with Abraham Robinson, a friend of Rabinowitch's parents. It was Robinson, who was a mathematician, logician, engineer, and also an art enthusiast, who introduced the artist to jazz and bebop music (Thelonious Monk, Bud Powell, Charlie Parker, John Coltrane, Oscar Pettiford, Wilbur Ware, Max Roach, and Shadow Wilson). Drawing upon his own experiences, Robinson encouraged Rabinowitch to cross-fertilize his knowledge acquired in the fields of the history of music, the history of science, and art history, and to forge a transdisciplinary thought. The artist is quick to acknowledge the role played by his mentor, citing the importance for him of bibliographical suggestions such as Erwin Panofsky's *Perspective as Symbolic Form* and *Early Netherlandish Painting*, and Alexandre Koyré's *From the Closed World to the Infinite Universe*.[3]

Finally, if we are to believe Roland Nachtigäller who reports having heard Rabinowitch confess that his "first encounter with modern art was when he saw Man Ray's photographic studies of mathematical models from the collection of the Henri Poincaré Institute in Paris,"[4] it becomes quite clear that Rabinowitch's initiation to art and to the sciences in these early years had a crucial and determining influence on the extremely methodical approach that was to make the artist's work unique.

A Question of Homages and "Judgements"

Later, in 1962, Rabinowitch began his series of homages to the masters of jazz and contemporary sculpture, putting forward not only his admiration for these tutelary figures but also his "judgements" with regard to their work. The term "judgement" is, in fact, used equally in the titles of his works and in the texts that accompany them, and it makes an important contribution to our understanding of his creative approach. Far from adhering to the image of the inspired artist, Rabinowitch acts rather as a logician, interpreting forms through a process of thought, and with the goal of questioning scientific data. For example, *3rd Homage to Jazz Drummers (for Max Roach). 3rd Judgement on Origins of Abstract Thinking* (fig. 1) is a sculpture made of two pieces of rusted steel that perfectly expresses these first experimentations. In this piece, the artist makes his homage to Max Roach in a work that is inspired by the axiomatic method in mathematics, and that deals with abstract thought through a conic form. The work develops a non-figurative geometrical construction in order to create a space of concrete experience in which the viewer can perceive the physical presence of the object, and, at the same time, imagine its abstract extension.[5] The homage to jazz drummers, something that does not appear to be obvious at first sight, is however justified by Rabinowitch himself when he writes:

> To me, the most fundamental and powerful expression of clear thinking in the realm of the concrete came from the actively working great jazz drummers of the day, also it seemed to me that a conic rose and fell like the sound of a drum.[6]

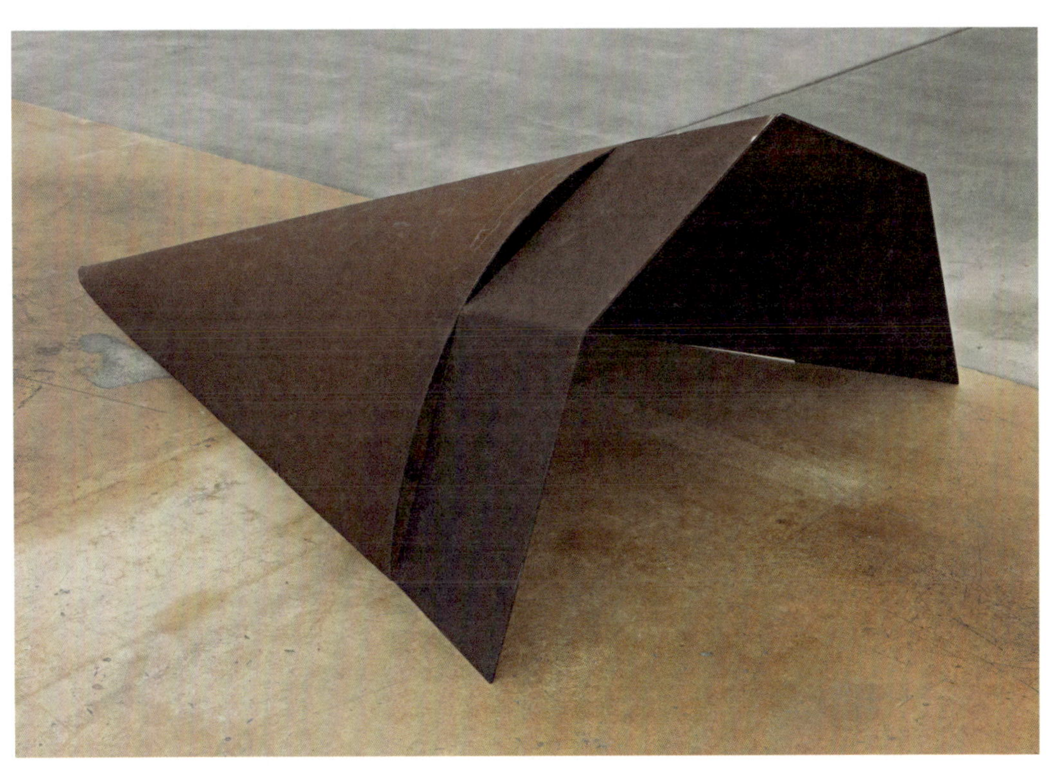

Fig. 1 *3rd Homage to Jazz Drummers: For Max Roach*, 1962
3rd Judgment on Origins of Abstract Thinking
Series: HOMAGES TO JAZZ DRUMMERS
(JUDGMENTS ON ORIGINS OF ABSTRACT THINKING)
two-piece sculpture, rusted steel, 73.5 × 225 × 144.5 cm (entire work),
MAMCO collection, gift of Max Wandeler

Accompanying this scientific approach, therefore, is a very subjective play of associations in which the study of mathematics is put into relation with a whole universe of references that derive almost exclusively from the artist's own biography, and notably from his relations with Abraham Robinson. It was at precisely this moment, in parallel with his dialogues with jazz, that Rabinowitch decided also to solidify the foundation of his thinking through confrontation with the history of sculpture in the 20th century. Between 1962 and 1965, the artist produced homages to David Smith, Aleksandr Rodchenko, Alberto Giacometti, Vladimir Tatlin, and Constantin Brancusi. The most well-documented of these are the *Five Addresses to Giacometti's "Le Nez" (Five Judgements On The Basis of Abstract Thinking)*, and, in particular, one of the most significant examples of his approach, *1st Address to "le Nez" (B): Central Order of Things and Events. 1st Judgement On The Basis of Abstract Thinking (1962)* (fig. 2). For Rabinowitch, Giacometti is the last Western sculptor to have had recourse to a figurative sculptural language still attached to some sort of realism—a language that Rabinowitch considered authentic in that Giacometti had explored exhaustively the many formal solutions offered by structural treatments of the human body, and his search for the perfect figurative expression had led to the recognition of the evolutive powerlessness of this language, explaining thus the transition to non-anthropomorphic solutions.[7] Giacometti's "*Le Nez* (The Nose)" is something of a case study for Rabinowitch because, in referring to it, he intends above all to demonstrate the spatial limits that the sculpture confronts, i.e. the impossibility of conceiving whole bodies on the basis of rational hypotheses. Following this principle, "*Le Nez*" would suggest the disembodiment of all anthropomorphic considerations having to do with the construction of works that address and call into question the body. Giacometti would thus, in Rabinowitch's reading, have created the very last example possible of figurative sculpture. At the same time, it seems that Rabinowitch himself, in his address

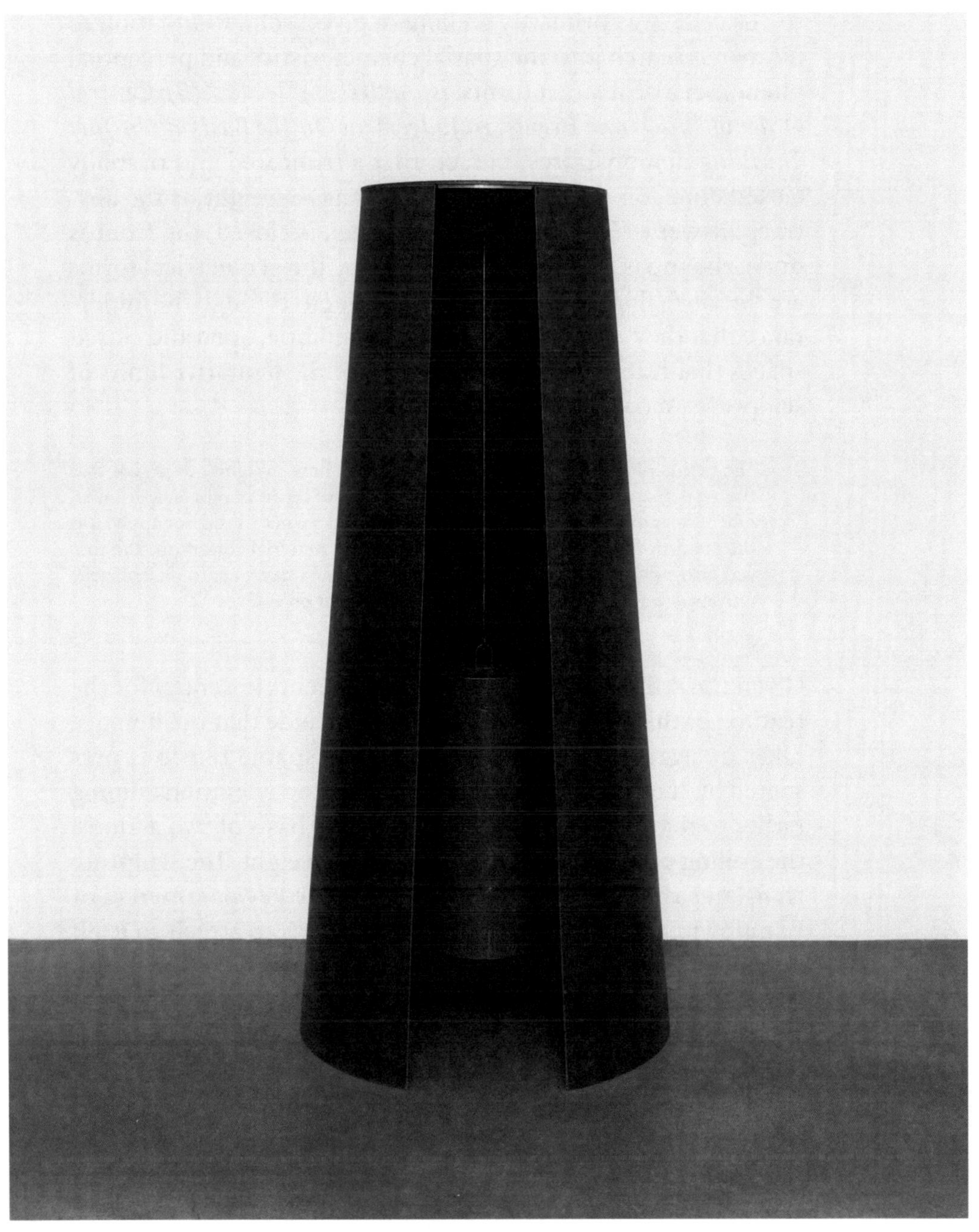

Fig. 2 *Initial Address to "Le Nez" (C): Central Order of Things and Events,* 1962
1st Judgment on the Basis of Abstract Thinking
Series: FIVE ADDRESSES TO GIACOMETTI'S "LE NEZ"
(FIVE JUDGMENTS ON THE BASIS OF ABSTRACT THINKING)
three-piece sculpture, oiled steel, cone: 178.5 (height) × 80 cm (diameter) / rod: 91 cm (length) × 1 cm (diameter) / weight: 59 cm (length) × 25.5 cm (diameter), MAMCO collection, gift of Max Wandeler

to "*Le Nez*," was primarily seeking to give a solid foundation to his own research into the spatial characteristics and perceptual phenomena of abstract forms. *1st Address to "le Nez" (B): Central Order of Things and Events. 1st Judgement On The Basis of Abstract Thinking* demonstrates, in fact, that a truncated and partially closed cone, on the inside of which hangs a weight, is the abstract answer to "Le Nez." Here, the back is closed, the front is open, the top is different to the bottom. The geometrical forms are thus in dialogue with those of Giacometti through the importance that they attach to the weights, equilibria, open and closed spaces that translate the overstepping of the figurative limits of sculpture. According to Rabinowitch,

> The title is Einstein's description of God, used here to signify to myself that the act of material acceptance, i.e. the rejection of the lie of representation or, much the same thing, the rejection of the rational where it did not apply, was the condition for establishing a fresh moral or material condition. The title was also a judgement and ironical, as its original intent, i.e. to describe the universal, was here applied to one rather peculiar object.[8]

Given the reflexive nature of these statements (essential for the reading of this work), it is possible to conclude that the homage takes up again, and with conviction, the spatial tensions presented by "Le Nez" in order to further develop operations aiming rather to redefine the formal moves on the basis of two actions: the coiling of a cone and the hanging of a weight. The sculpture translates thus, in an eruptive fashion, the key parameters of Rabinowitch's artistic thought, and it seems to attach to itself the thoughts of one of the protagonists of the history of art of the past century.[9]

Barrels and Cones

Royden Rabinowitch has ceaselessly renewed his research into sculpture, and he has done so above all by deepening his understanding of abstract/geometrical space and the ordinary space of our experience as these spaces are defined in the thought of Henri Poincaré. In parallel with this, the artist has created objects that seek to interrogate the perceptual dynamics that govern the relations between the observer's body and perceived objects. If the movement and the experience of the viewer allow for the understanding of the abstract and ordinary space created through contact with the sculptural object, Royden Rabinowitch's work, with its forms consciously inspired by mathematical theories, aims to appeal to the totality of the viewer's perceptual fields.[10] Hence, out of this concern there follows another series of "judgements" that the artist begins to formulate, after 1960, on such well-known contemporary sculptors as Anthony Caro and Donald Judd. The former was the object of a form of criticism that analyzed his works reductively down to an attempt to draw an abstract landscape. Royden Rabinowitch fastened upon Michael Fried's interpretation of Caro's sculptures in the 1960s[11] in which Fried insists upon the importance of abstraction in Caro, and stresses, above all, the extreme "opticality" of his objects—an opticality that was conditioned by an expressive pictorial syntax. The strong visual and multi-directional dimension of Caro's works, that Fried saw as akin to landscapes, would thus be a perceptual "mediator" between the work of sculpture and the viewer, in the same way that architecture was for Donald Judd.[12] According to Rabinowitch, therefore, the productions of these two artists were of primordial importance for art history; however, as a result of their being subject to the principle of landscape or architecture, they failed to engage fully with the complexity of spatial relations that should be the defining feature of contemporary sculpture. Donald Judd's work, staying as it did within the limits of rectilinear modules, reduced therefore, through the imposition of a particular orientation (a "specificity"[13]), the number of directions of his objects. This requirement went very much against Rabinowitch's approach to his own work, and, from 1975, the latter was to reject his affiliation with Minimalism. In that year, Donald Judd, in his studio in New York, said to Rabinowitch that given the serious interest that they both had taken, in the 1950s and independently one of the other, in David Smith's *Five Units Equal*, Rabinowitch's belonging to the movement seemed to be inevitable. Rabinowitch's rejection, however, rested upon a major objection: contrary to Judd's approach, his own interpretation of Smith's work had nothing to do with painting, and he forcefully denounced any type of "mediation" between the object and the viewer's body.[14]

Following his desire to go beyond Anthony Caro's "opticality" and Donald Judd's "specificity," the Canadian artist finally chose the barrel as his sculptural medium of choice. This allowed him, first of all, to use in his sculpture the double-curvature that we see in the barrel's structure, and it allowed him then to work with the full complexity of the spatial dynamics that were at the centre of his interest in mathematics and physics. He rebuilt, therefore, parts of disassembled barrels, using artisanal building methods in order to obtain an ensemble of forms laid out horizontally—flat and tectonic structures.[15] *Barrel Construction: Double Curvature at Right Angles* (fig. 3) from 1963, part of the series *Barrel Constructions—Double Curvatures at Right Angles (Construction of an internally determined non-anthropomorphic and non-articulated body)*, is a work that involves the creation of a form that is easily grasped by the observer as far as its own intentions are concerned, i.e. the internal spaces and component parts that determine its presence in a given space.[16] Royden Rabinowitch comments on this series, providing important details for its interpretation:

> I then thought that if I could reorient the parts of a barrel around a right angle the contradiction of those secondary suggestions would be obvious. I used the methods of construction that the barrel employed with no external means of joining. I then made a succession of moments or balances based on the dimensions of the members which, when finally collected together, completed the sculpture.[17]

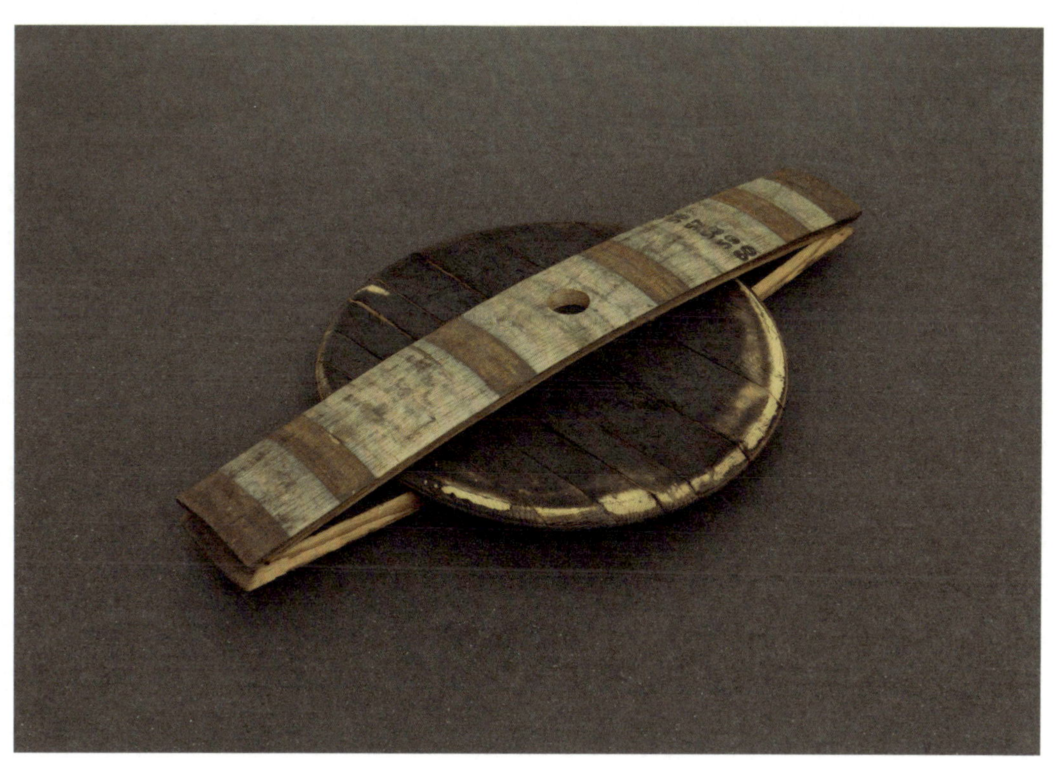

Fig. 3 *Barrel Construction (Double Curvature at Right Angles)*, 1963
Series: BARREL CONSTRUCTIONS—
DOUBLE CURVATURES AT RIGHT ANGLES
(CONSTRUCTION OF AN INTERNALLY DETERMINED NON-ANTHROPOMORPHIC NON-ARTICULATED BODY)
three-piece sculpture, oak barrel wood, 10 × 89 × 53 cm (entire work), MAMCO collection, gift of Max Wandeler

Ultimately, therefore, we find ourselves faced with an "action situation," and this gives us certainly access to the finished work, but it provides access also to the conceptual and material stages of its construction. The procedural dimension in art, claimed with some reticence by the artist in the form of a series of scientific deductions, seems to us, however, of great interest in connection with another series, namely the one devoted to *Greased Cones (1st Construction Regarding Internal Conditions)*. Two examples of this series, *Green Discrete Vertically Greased Cone* (fig. 4) and *Dark Grey Horizontally Greased Cone* (fig. 5) from 1965, show the various treatments of this form and its greasing, as indicated by the titles. These greased cones are part of Rabinowitch's research into the internal conditions of sculpture because the viewer can easily see that the greased surface of the cone hides, in reality, an internal structure that cannot maintain, all by itself, a straight line. Through the spreading of a greasy material on the steel surfaces, Rabinowitch disturbs the symmetrical quality of the geometrical figure, forcing us to interrogate its concrete properties, and to imagine the artist in an "action situation."[18] Rabinowitch is adamant about this aspect:

> The greasing allowed me to make asymmetrical a symmetrical condition because the grease could not be put on evenly. Because of this, it gave me an opportunity to emphasize location and action, i.e. my location and my action regarding the cone, at the same time. [...] Again, this sculpture was conceived of as a sequence of operations...[19]

In using the cone at the same time as did the Arte Povera artists, in particular Mario Merz, Rabinowitch was trying to alter our perception of it through the use of a material such as grease. During this same period, Joseph Beuys was also using grease. Yet, if Beuys was to use the suppleness of grease to test out its reactions, Royden Rabinowitch was less concerned with such questions, concentrating above all on making visible the internal potentialities of sculptural objects. Through barrels and cones, steel and grease, the artist was to develop an increasingly

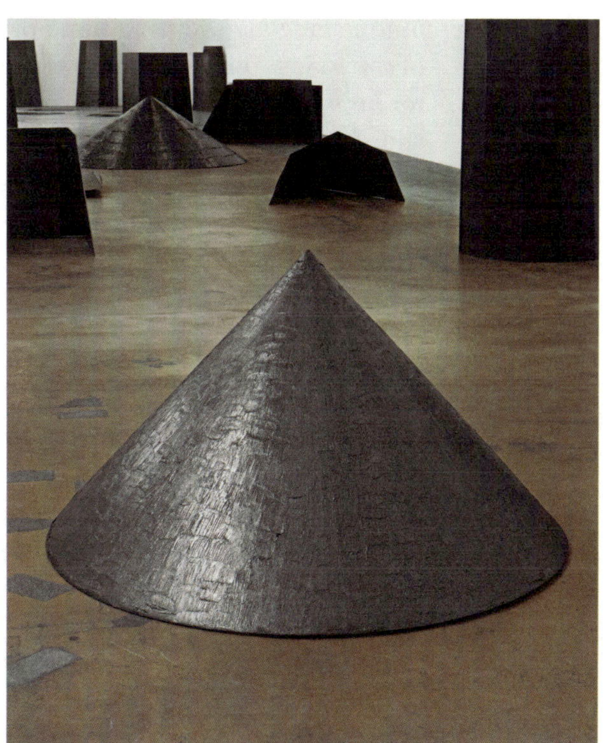

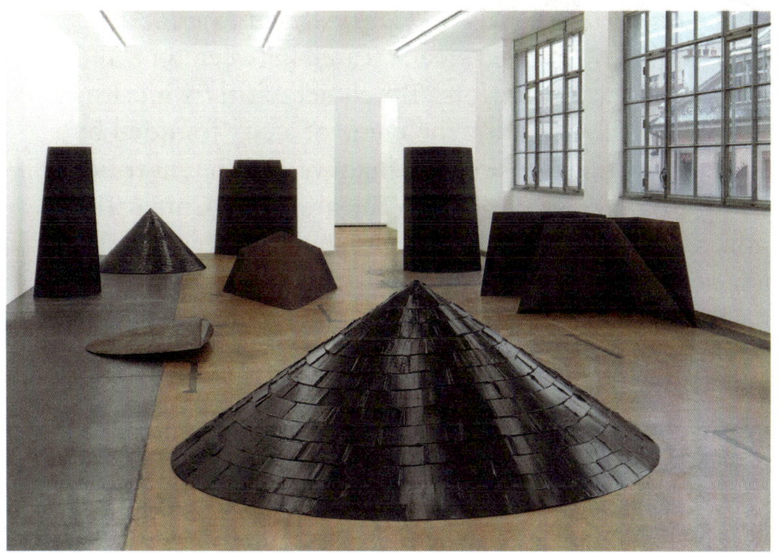

Fig. 4 *Discrete Green Vertically Greased Cone*, 1965
Series: GREASED CONES
(1ST CONSTRUCTION REGARDING INTERNAL CONDITIONS)
steel, grease, 120 cm (height) × 168 cm (diameter),
MAMCO collection, gift of Max Wandeler

Fig. 5 *Dark Grey Horizontally Greased Cone*, 1965
Series: GREASED CONES
(1ST CONSTRUCTION REGARDING INTERNAL CONDITIONS)
steel, grease, 105 (height) × 274 cm (diameter),
MAMCO collection, gift of Max Wandeler

unique language, setting him apart from the great movements of the 1960s. The year 1965 marks, indeed, a major turning point for his work—all of the foundations of his thought and work are laid. From this year on, he was to perfect, amplify and deepen the experiments that had led him to conceive a path of research, rigorous and demanding, into the relations between sculpture and the spaces of bodies.

Syntheses and Openings

At the beginning of the 1970s, Royden Rabinowitch appeared to have definitively found his direction, and it is precisely during this period that he felt the need to make a synthesis of his previous experimentations. He writes in this regard:

> I felt that I too had to synthesize or unite all the implications of the various constructions that I had previously made to have a chance of attacking a major sculptural assumption, i.e. the impossibility of making a fresh, i.e. more discrete, fully articulated body.[20]

The *Karakorum* series, *Synthetic Construction (Synthesis of Previous Work)* (fig. 6), in oiled steel, created between 1968 and 1971, materialized these ambitions. The choice of title, while ironic, is not banal. Karakorum is the name of a city founded by Genghis Khan for the purpose of uniting several different tribes under a single banner—a prelude to the attack on China. The name of the city, therefore, evokes the ensemble of Rabinowitch's judgements on the origins, developments, and bases of abstract thought, and on the implications of the purely internal conditions of sculptures. It represents a distancing from the attitude of searching for freedom vis-à-vis the "fathers," and it bears witness to the inauguration of a new chapter that will demonstrate a solidly acquired autonomy and maturity. From this moment on, Rabinowitch, as a Post-minimalist, was to claim that contemporary sculpture had a duty to confront, through its play of

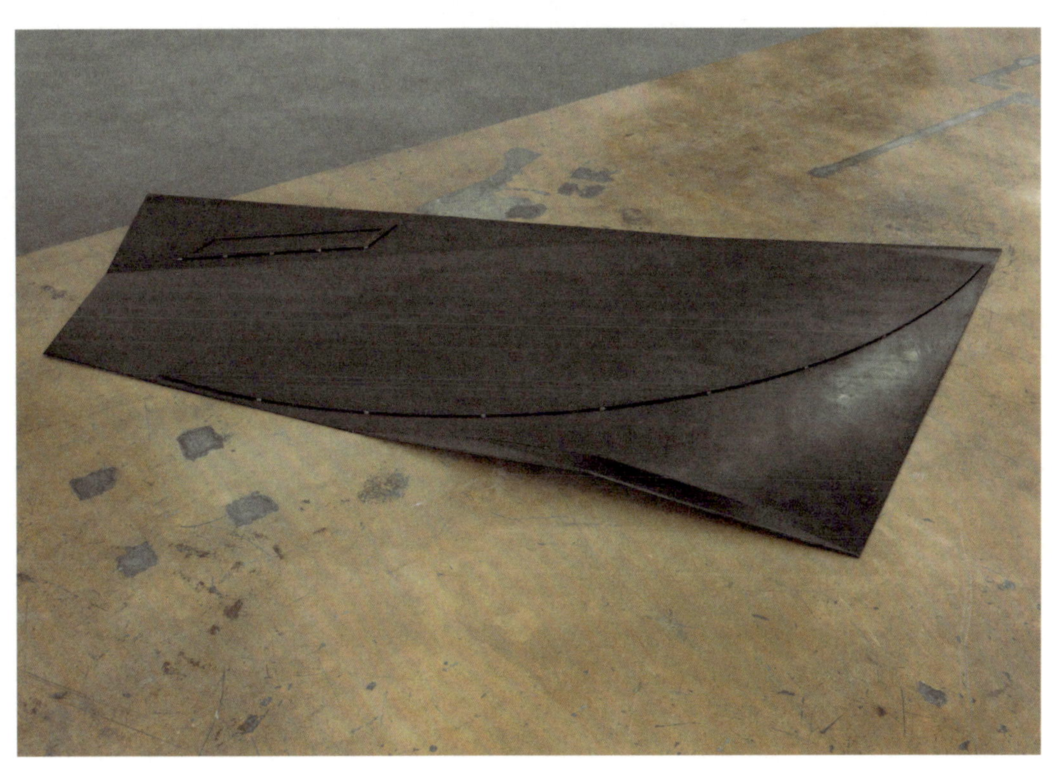

Fig. 6 *Karakorum (IV)*, 1968–1971
Series: KARAKORUM – SYNTHETIC CONSTRUCTION
(SYNTHESIS OF PREVIOUS WORK)
oiled steel, 7 × 162 × 290 cm, MAMCO collection, gift of Max Wandeler

volumes, the entirety of bodily sensations, and that it was duty bound to distance itself from a uniquely optical perception, an approach that had been excessively stressed, as he saw it, by Minimalism. By placing the body at the center of the sculptural environment, the artist was aiming to provoke a physical disturbance while, at the same time, stressing the autonomy of the work. It was precisely this apparently irreconcilable relationship that he was seeking to explore. This was his response to the critique put forward by the art historian Michael Fried in *Art and Objecthood*.[21] Fried had attacked the "theatrical" dimension of Minimalist art, and, more generally, the theatricality of all reductive aesthetics. In this famous text, Fried stressed the importance that the Minimalist artists accorded to the viewer's experience rather than to the inner relational properties of the works. Living and working far from the world's art capitals, Royden Rabinowitch evidently took no part in these debates, yet he was probing deeply into questions of gravity, spatial orientation, specificity of the site, and the relations between the interior and exterior of sculpture, in order to reach an understanding of the physical experience of spaces that are not connected visually. He was developing thus a response to Michael Fried's argument, a response that had much in common with Richard Serra's research, yet without an engagement with radical experimentation on materials, and maintaining above all a mastery of created volumes.[22] Furthermore, the two artists shared a sensitivity to the forces acting upon objects, and to the relations between the spaces they create through their contact with the ground; however, unlike Richard Serra, Rabinowitch was never seeking to test out the limits of the sculptural gesture. He kept, rather, to mathematical deductions applied to steel sheets, that he bent with manual presses, and it is this work that earned him, at the beginning of the 1980s, real recognition through the exhibition *Spuren, Skulpturen und Monumente ihrer präzisen Reise*,[23] directed by Harald Szeemann at the Kunsthaus in Zurich. During this period, Rabinowitch's work was extremely well-received in

Europe, to the extent that he had several solo shows, the most significant of which being the 1984 exhibition instigated by Jan Hoet at the Museum van Hedendaagse Kunst in Ghent, and the 1985 show at the Städtisches Museum Abteiberg in Mönchengladbach organized by Johannes Cladders. Through his contribution to the postmodernist tendency that Rosalind Krauss, in her article "Sculpture in the Expanded Field,"[24] situated at the origin of the expansion of the fields of sculpture, Rabinowitch pursued, in an original fashion, his explorations into the internal conditions of sculpture. He subjected his production to a series of calculations that underlay volumes allowing the observer to perceive their internal characteristics as determined by the high and the low, right and left, foreground and background, open and closed angles, as well as being governed by a sensitivity to orientations and the oblique line, to the vertical and the horizontal in equal measure with formal rhythms.[25] This openness to science and to the determinist approach of spatial possibilities implicitly implied a distancing of the artist with regard to the artwork. Yet this was always done as part of a desire for shared experience; the viewer's body is understood not only as a basic point of reference, but also as a determining element for the existence of the new, enlarged spaces of sculpture, to the extent that the object's beauty clearly appears to be of lesser importance than the calculated form.

The Multifarious Languages of Sculpture

In the MAMCO's collection, we find a significant number of objects that were created from the early 1980s onwards. The majority of these works have as their starting point the series of *Manifolds*, that includes *7 Manifolds in 4 Locations with Varied Handed Additions* (fig. 7) from 1986, a piece belonging to the series *2ND Internally Determined Fully Articulated Body (Handed Manifold Groups—General Cases of Handed Developed Surfaces*

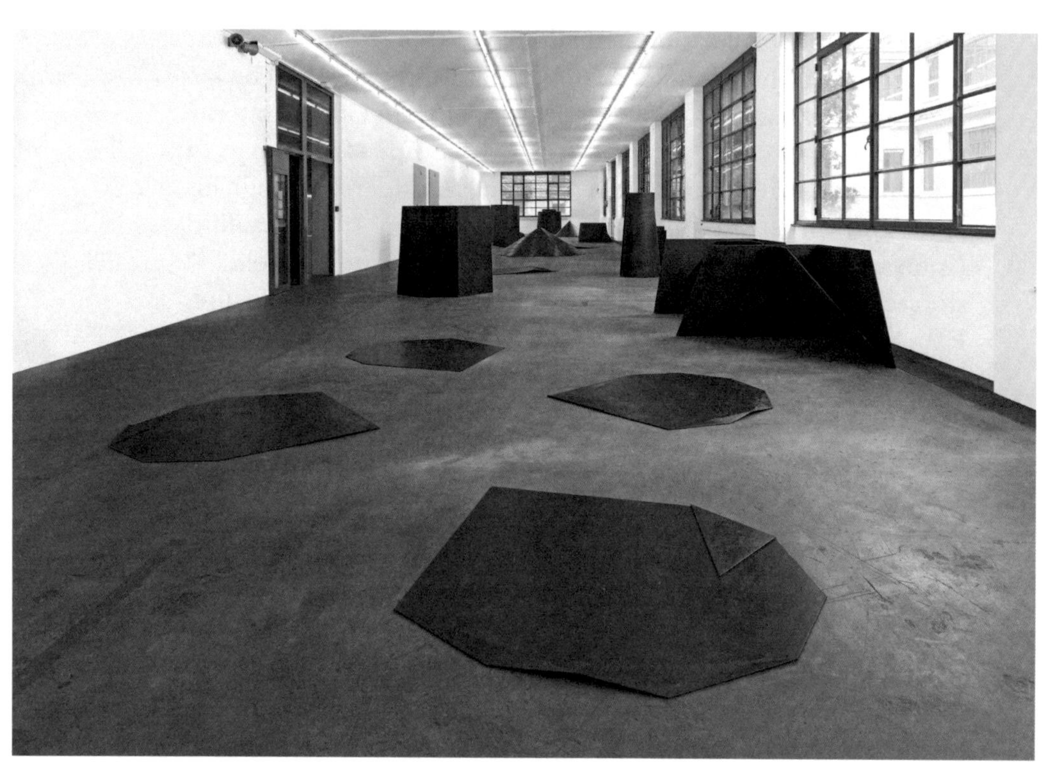

Fig. 7 *7 Manifolds in 4 Locations with Varied Handed Additions*, 1986
Series: 2ND INTERNALLY DETERMINED FULLY ARTICULATED BODY (HANDED MANIFOLD GROUPS – GENERAL CASES OF HANDED DEVELOPED SURFACES OF ONE SIZE APPLIED TO PLANS) MAINTAINING LOCAL SOMATIC DESCRIPTIONS
four-piece sculpture, blackened and oiled steel, 2 × [2.5 × 132.5 × 116 cm] / 2.5 × 130.5 × 115.5 cm / 2.5 × 130.7 × 118.5 cm, MAMCO collection, gift of Max Wandeler

of One Size Applied to Plans). It seems to us, therefore, of crucial importance that, by way of conclusion, we make clear the basis on which this new chapter was to develop—a chapter firmly anchored in research into the *Manifolds*, sculptures that the artist has defined as "unified entities in parts." As their title suggests, these forms assume multiple parts with the aim of addressing the entirety of the identities that a body might potentially reveal in situations of observation. Rabinowitch explains it thus:

> They suggest that location or the space of the observer is not separate from objects, that location is not separate from actual identity. The construction stresses that, as the body takes up new locations, the body drastically changes, so that although external similarities seem to apply, physical states are totally changed, hence, a manifold exactly the same as another manifold, in a different location, with a different orientation, with a different handed element added to a different facet, will make totally new demands on observers...[26]

In an effort to make his work more accessible, Rabinowitch has often used the following anecdote about a cat as a pragmatic explanation of the multiple constraints arising from our experience of the sculptures. The story goes back to 1978, and the occasion was the artist's first solo exhibition at the John Weber Gallery in New York. As Rabinowitch tells it, a cat had begun to walk across the gallery, but the animal suddenly stopped, walked around one of the *Manifolds*, and sat down in front of its openings. The cat, attracted by this space, patiently waited for many minutes.[27] For Rabinowitch, this reaction was proof of the space-structuring dimension of the objects and of our own "primitive" experience of them. The story also allows us to take our distance from the artist's sophisticated mathematical calculations and to validate the immediacy of an instinctive reaction, namely one that places an animal body before the spaces created by the *Manifolds*.[28] At issue here is an attempt to describe the spatial quality of the "perceived" world, involving equally objects and our own bodies, and consequently the whole of the "spatialities" generated by their interrelations. If it is true that Royden Rabinowitch's constructions are primarily reflections on space and on its development as a concept, what they ultimately produce, through their contact with observers, are concrete and understandable spaces. One can say, following Jaromir Jedlinski, that Rabinowitch's intellectual approach is very much like Ludwig Wittgenstein's analysis of "language games." Accordingly, Rabinowitch can be seen as an artist who describes and classifies certain rules of the language of sculpture.[29] Description and classification are, in fact, omnipresent in his approach to his work, and we see this in his long and complex titles—rather than offering descriptions of the content of the works, they are more akin to provable theorems. In much the same way as with Umberto Boccioni's titles, the title of a work, for Rabinowitch, is not simply a description of the real appearance of the object; it contributes, rather, in an essential way to the process of construction of spaces, reaffirming thus the necessity of our own experience of the work, i.e. the work's "proof" through the observer's own bodily experience of it. As Rabinowitch put it, "I read these titles as operational methods as well as poems of material necessity."[30]

Without actually using the term "theorem" here, the artist is stressing the material need for a theoretical method by placing it at the very centre of the construction of his objects and drawings. This aspect confirms that, between language and experience, the constellation of works created by Rabinowitch has evolved in a context that has always made possible the testing out of contemporary spatialities. His entire work has been developed and realized alongside the great movements of the second half of the last century, bringing to them a precise, rigorous, and extremely generous reflection.

Notes

1 Rudi Fuchs, "Royden Rabinowitch" in *Royden Rabinowitch. Sculpture and Drawing 1992/1993*, Exh. cat., (Zurich: Haus für Konstruktive und Konkrete Kunst, 1993), p. 8.

2 Roman Kurzmeyer, "Royden Rabinowitch" in *Royden Rabinowitch. Ghent*, Exh. cat., (Gand: Mer Paper Kunsthalle, 2014), p. 6.

3 Royden Rabinowitch, "Het Lam Gods & The Content of My Art," ibid., p.43–44.

4 Roland Nachtigäller, "Forward," trans. Chris Abbey, in Royden Rabinowitch, Exh. cat., (Herford: Marta Herford, 2009), p. 5.

5 Roman Kurzmeyer, "Royden Rabinowitch," in *Royden Rabinowitch. Ghent*, op. cit., p. 14.

6 Royden Rabinowitch, "Collected Notes," in *Royden Rabinowitch, Sculpture 1962/1992*, (The Hague: Gemeentemuseum, 1992), p. 352.

7 Jaromir Jedlinski, "Sculptural Investigations," in *Royden Rabinowitch, Skulpturen 1990*, Exh. cat., (Bern: Kunstmuseum, 1990), p. 54–55.

8 Royden Rabinowitch, "Collected Notes," in *Royden Rabinowitch, Sculpture 1962/1992*, op. cit., p. 355.

9 Roland Nachtigäller, "The Anatomy of Perception–On Royden Rabinowitch," in *Royden Rabinowitch. Ghent*, op. cit., p. 38.

10 Elisabeth Grossmann, "On New Works by Royden Rabinowitch," in *Royden Rabinowitch. Sculpture and Drawing 1992/1993*, op. cit., p. 5.

11 See Michael Fried, *Anthony Caro: Sculpture 1960–1963*, (London: Whitechapel Art Gallery, 1963).

12 Roman Kurzmeyer, "Royden Rabinowitch," in *Royden Rabinowitch. Ghent*, op. cit., p. 16.

13 See Donald Judd, "Specific Objects," *Arts Yearbook*, no 8, 1965, pp. 74–82

14 Royden Rabinowitch, "Het Lam Gods & The Content of My Art," op. cit., p. 48.

15 Roman Kurzmeyer, "Artists, Bodies, Observers and Space: Relations in Royden Rabinowitch's work," in *Royden Rabinowitch, Skulpturen 1990*, op. cit., p. 22.

16 David Bellman, "The 'Barrel Constructions' of Royden Rabinowitch: Their Meaning and Effect," in *Royden Rabinowitch, Sculptures and Drawings in the Collection*, op. cit., pp. 21–22.

17 Royden Rabinowitch, "Collected Notes," in *Royden Rabinowitch. Sculpture and Drawing 1992/1993*, op. cit., p. 359.

18 Jan Hoet, *The Sculptures of Royden Rabinowitch—a Discovery*, in *Royden Rabinowitch, Sculptures and Drawings in the Collection*, Exh. cat., (Ghent: Museum van Hedendaagse Kunst, 1984), p. 17.

19 Royden Rabinowitch, "Collected Notes," in *Royden Rabinowitch. Sculpture and Drawing 1992/1993*, op. cit., p. 362.

20 Ibid., p. 368.

21 Michael Fried, "Art and Objecthood," *Artforum*, vol. 5, no 10, 1967, pp. 12–23.

22 Roman Kurzmeyer, Royden Rabinowitch, in *Royden Rabinowitch. Ghent*, op. cit., p. 16.

23 See *Spuren, Skulpturen und Monumente ihrer präzisen Reise*, Exh. cat., (Zurich: Kunsthaus, 1985).

24 Rosalind Krauss, "Sculpture in the Expanded Field," *October*, vol. 8, 1979, pp. 30–44.

25 *Spuren, Skulpturen und Monumente ihrer präzisen Reise*, op. cit., p. 102.

26 Royden Rabinowitch, "Collected Notes," in *Royden Rabinowitch. Sculpture and Drawing 1992/1993*, op. cit., p. 391–392.

27 Roman Kurzmeyer, *Royden Rabinowitch*, in *Royden Rabinowitch. Ghent*, op. cit., p. 10.

28 I am grateful to the artist Arnaud Vassaux for having made me aware of this notion.

29 Jaromir Jedlinski, *Sculptural Investigations*, in *Royden Rabinowitch, Skulpturen 1990*, op. cit., p. 52.

30 Royden Rabinowitch, "Collected Notes," in *Royden Rabinowitch, Sculpture 1962/1992*, op. cit., p. 349.

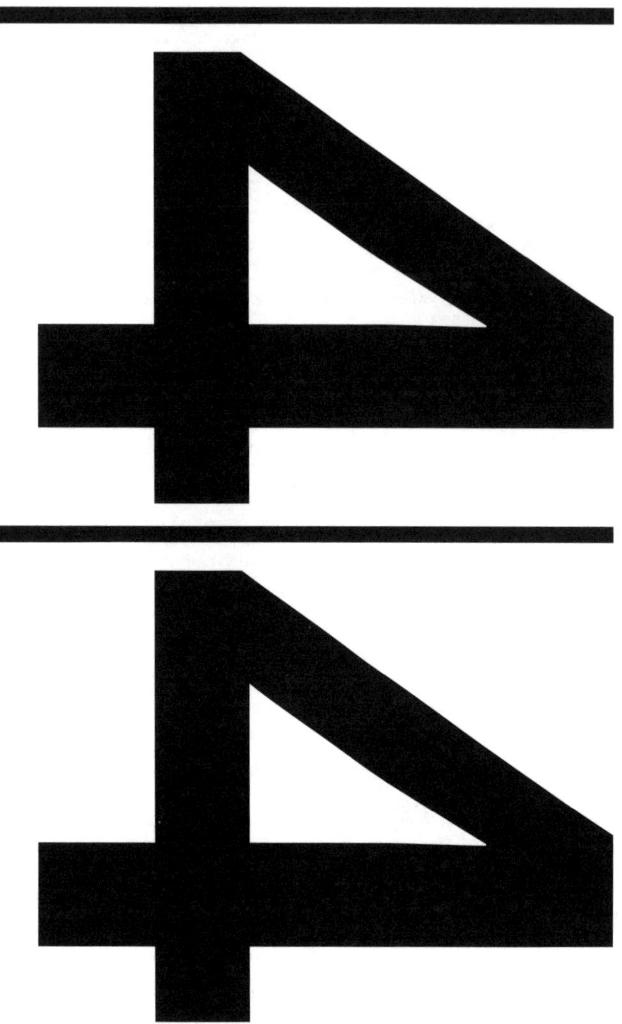

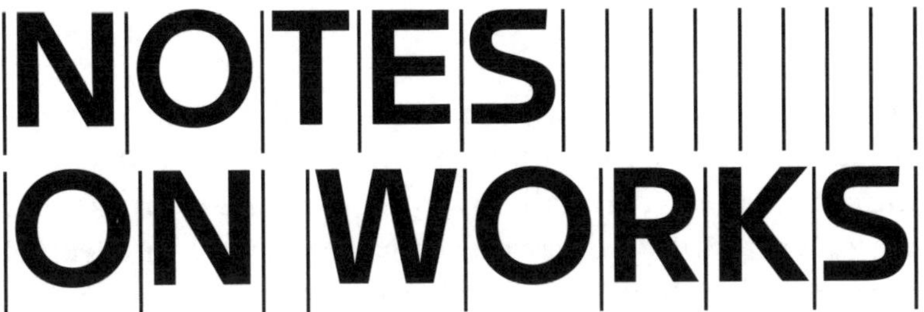

Sophie Costes

Introduction

Starkly beautiful and possessing a sober restraint, a "formal ascesis" even, that has led to its having been wrongly associated with Minimalist art, Royden Rabinowitch's work arises from deep erudition in art, music, literature, and also science—intellectual explorations that the artist began between the years 1962 (when he was only 20 years old) and 1965, in Toronto. To paraphrase Tony Smith, Rabinowitch's sculptures, created on a human scale, are made neither to dominate nor to be dominated by the one who looks at them; they invite the observer, rather, to enter into a dialogue. They belong to a current running counter to a tendency seen in part of the new sculpture of their time, a tendency that, as Robert Morris explained it, stressed enormous size in order to avoid intimacy.[1] Rabinowitch's works do not go so far as to invalidate Lessing's statement that "sculpture is an art concerned with the deployment of bodies in space;"[2] however, their anthropomorphic quality is subtly allusive, the bodies in question are both that of the artist and the viewer, including the latter's "consciousness of his own time as he experiences the work,"[3]—a shared experience, therefore, involving both the work and the viewer.

Existing "at the juncture of stillness and motion,"[4] these works take up various positions in the exhibition space. They are positioned up against or hanging on the wall, parallel or perpendicular to it, or adopting almost the flatness of the floor. The sculptures are composed of single, dual, or quadruple pieces, or groupings of six. Along with these variations, the artist uses a wide variety of materials: grease, wood, aluminum, steel (oiled, rusted, or blued), and his works are built of both newly-made sections and pre-existing parts such as barrel staves and covers. His sculptures include surfaces that are open, closed, twinned, vertical, horizontal, hollow or concave, that, through his work with the hand press,[5] extend from flat plane to volume, and involve bending, rolling, cutting, and, very rarely, welding. Materials and forms are added, rarely subtracted. The dominant medium is steel, as it was for the sculptor David Smith, a metallurgist and habitué of scrap yards,[6] whose artistic production has been unavoidable for Rabinowitch since the latter's discovery of it in 1957. Most of Rabinowitch's works are in series (*works in progress*), or to use Jaromir Jedlinski's expression, they are "sculptural investigations."[7]

In his sculpture and drawing, Rabinowitch engages in a struggle against (scientific) idealism, leading him to distinguish the view of any local/somatic operator (the observer) with that of any rational/empirical operator (the scientist). He makes this contrast by means of a constantly recurring basic figure, a "concrete model of the rational/empirical operator: the cone within a cylinder of equal base and height."[8] Rabinowitch establishes thus a confrontation between the judgment of abstract thought and the direct experience of the work. At intervals throughout the artist's work, there are "Addresses" to Tatlin, Giacometti, Brancusi, as well as homages to classical musicians and to the exponents of free jazz. His oeuvre is autonomous and unclassifiable; arising in parallel with Minimalist and Post-minimalist art, it is very much part of the revival of sculpture in the 20th century. And we must add, to the aforementioned pantheon, Poincaré's *Science and Hypothesis*, a text that, when he discovered it, marked a turning point in Rabinowitch's life, giving his work a practical objective, anchoring it firmly in relation with the here and now: "a search for the directly constructible equivalent of Poincaré's description of the space of ordinary experience."[9]

In this complex, hieratic, and rigorous oeuvre, Jonathan Swift's "excremental vision" and his critique of science (based on the idea that nature is not perfectible), along with the comic duo Stan Laurel and Oliver Hardy,[10] are salutary counterpoints to what the artist sees as the excess and misdirection of science when used in the service of a totalitarian idea. The titles of his works, essentially descriptive, and suggesting an intimate knowledge of each work, are often hard to navigate, combining terms from a glossary that is poetic and unique to the artist.[11]

From quite early on, Rabinowitch's sculptures were to find a ready reception in Switzerland. The very first exhibition of his work was at the 3rd of the *Salons de galeries-pilotes* in Lausanne in 1970, and this was followed by shows at the Kunsthaus in Zürich (1985), in Bern (1990)—the city where Einstein had formulated his theory of relativity—and at the Haus für Konstruktive und Konkrete Kunst in Zürich (1992/1993). In addition to these exhibitions, there was the *in-situ* installation *Three Rolled Conic Surfaces of One Size Applied To a Region of Curvature Maintaining Local Somatic Descriptions* (1987) at the Furka Pass in the Swiss Alps, a location whose mountainous terrain and enveloping surround offered plunging views down into the valley below.[12]

Exhibited at the very first opening of the MAMCO in September 1994, the works assembled and deposited at the museum through the good judgment and perspicacity of Max Wandeler, have been shown there regularly since 1994, and they became, by way of a gift on his part, officially part of the collection in 2016.

Glossary

Articulated: "... some clear description of bodily action. All figurative and anthropomorphic bodies describe human action in terms of external morphology."[13]

Internal physical conditions: "... physical conditions obscured by surfaces but none the less knowable through observation of the construction."[14]

Developed: bent (from 2 to 3 dimensions).

Dimensional ordinary space: the ordinary space of experience.[15]

Somatic properties: "properties that a conscious body becomes aware of when it moves in space."[16]

Somatic: "These so-called somatic properties can be listed as follows: the closed/open and front/back property; the handed (i.e. right or left) quality; a sense of all the directions, oblique, vertical and horizontal; total asymmetry of the observer's body with its heart beating on the left; the top/bottom property, the top being different from the bottom."[17]

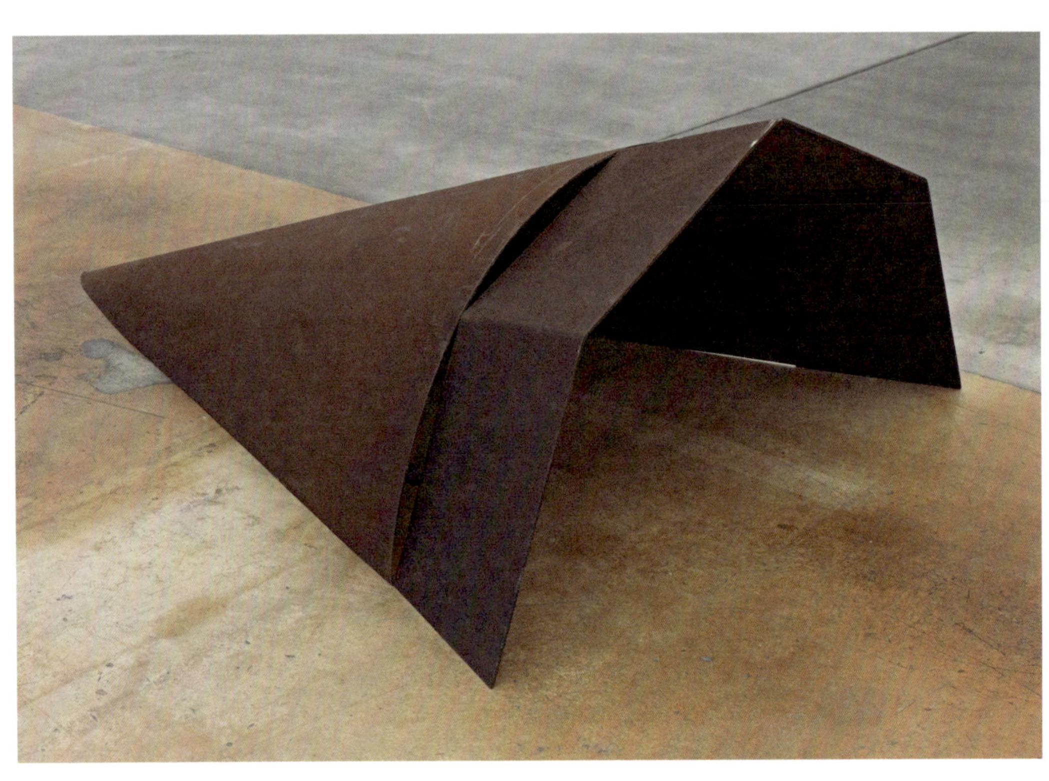

3rd Homage to Jazz Drummers: For Max Roach, 1962
3rd Judgment on Origins of Abstract Thinking
Series: HOMAGES TO JAZZ DRUMMERS
(JUDGMENTS ON ORIGINS OF ABSTRACT THINKING)
two-piece sculpture, rusted steel
73.5 × 225 × 144.5 cm (entire work)
MAMCO collection, gift of Max Wandeler
inv.: 2016–417 (1 to 2)

The homages to classical and jazz musicians who revolutionized their discipline occur at intervals in Rabinowitch's work. In this series of sculptures devoted to jazz drummers, each work being composed of two more or less disconnected pieces, Rabinowitch takes the conic as his basis. The homage to Max Roach[18] takes the form of a truncated half-cone with four sides, inserted into, and extended by, a plain, non-truncated half-cone.[19] The steel used here is a steel devoid of surface treatment, and to which rust, much-valued by the pioneers of metal sculpture in the 1950s, gives a particular color and patina, all the while being suggestive of the world of industry. [20]

The fact that Max Roach was a drummer is relevant here. The sculpture is built up through the addition of parts: horizontally reclining half-cones. The volume of the sculpture is hollow. It is like a drum covered with a metallic skin, marking out the internal space of the sculpture and space of the observer. As the artist explains it: "To me, the most fundamental and powerful expression of clear thinking in the realm of the concrete came from the actively working great jazz drummers of the day, also it seemed to me that a conic rose and fell like the sound of a drum.[21]"

This third homage to jazz drummers[22] takes the form of a domestic "monument"—evocative of Vladimir Tatlin's *Monument to the Third International*—arranged here horizontally by Rabinowitch a few years before Carl Andre was to use the same procedure to lay Brancusi's *Endless Column* against the ground.

With this series of sculptures, we see one of the first instances where Rabinowitch explicitly refers to abstract thought, its origins in Greece, and to speculations that are theoretical, arbitrary, and unverifiable because they go beyond the range of experience, and are linked to the discovery of incommensurability in music and mathematics.[23]

Exhibition history

Rudiments d'un musée possible 1 – September 23, 1994–January 29, 1995
Rudiments d'un musée possible 2 – February 17, 1995–May 30, 1995
L'Éternel Détour – Summer sequence 2011 – Presentation of the collections 2011 (Summer) – June 8, 2011–September 18, 2011

Bibliography

Royden Rabinowitch, *Works 1962–1995*, Exh. cat., (Lodz: Muzeum Sztuki, 1995), pp. 51–57, ill. p. 57 #6.
Rabinowitch, Sculpture 1962–1992, Exh. cat., (The Hague: Gemeentemuseum, 1992), ill. pp. 19–21 #3.

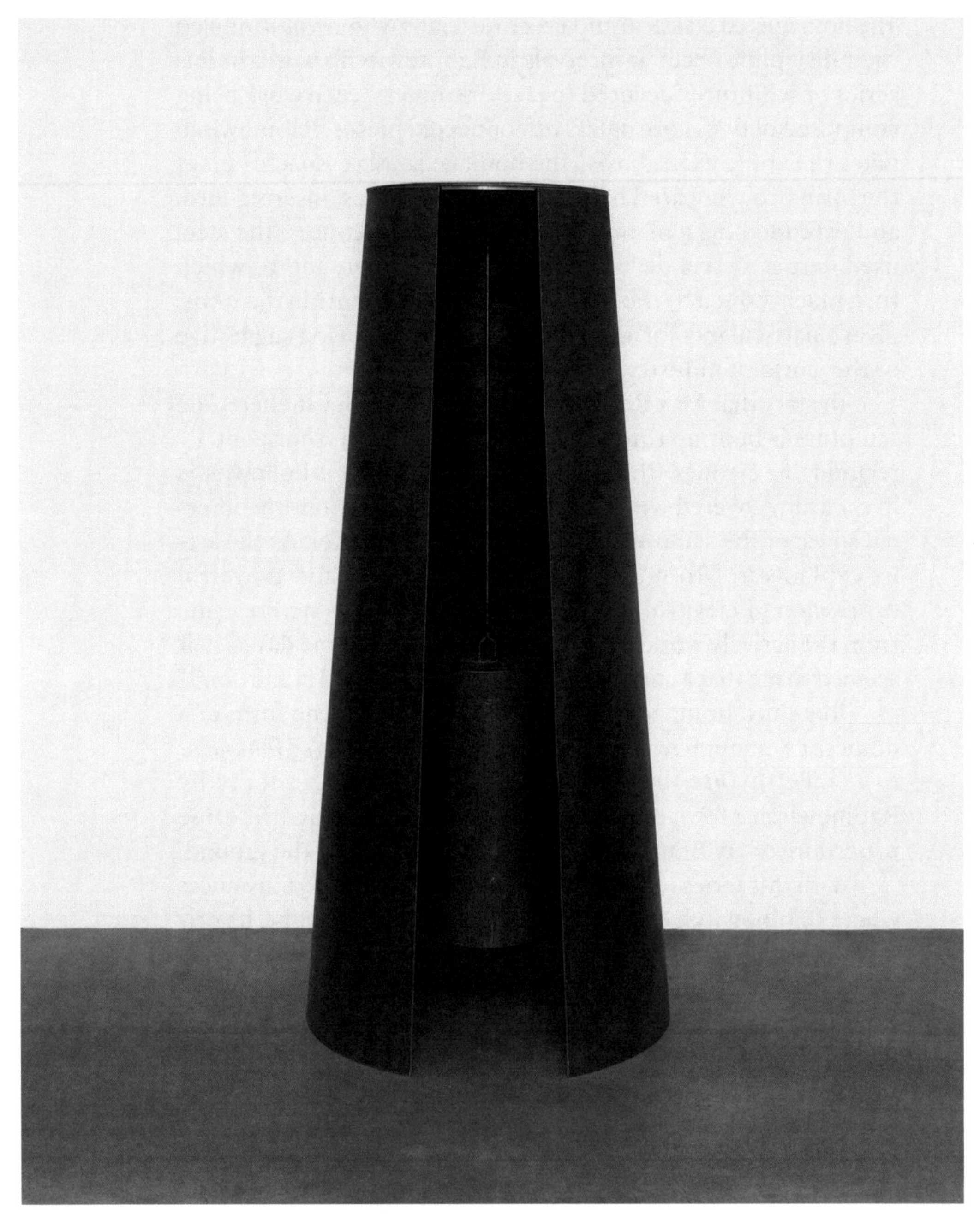

Initial Address to "Le Nez" (C): Central Order of Things and Events, 1962
1st Judgment on the Basis of Abstract Thinking
Series: FIVE ADDRESSES TO GIACOMETTI'S "LE NEZ"
(FIVE JUDGMENTS ON THE BASIS OF ABSTRACT THINKING)
three-piece sculpture, oiled steel
cone: 178.5 (height) × 80 cm (diameter) / rod: 91 cm (length) × 1 cm (diameter) / weight: 59 cm (length) × 25.5 cm (diameter)
MAMCO collection, gift of Max Wandeler
inv.: 2016–420 (1 to 3)

This sculpture, composed of two main parts, includes a frame—a truncated, partially closed cone—on the inside of which a brown cylinder hangs on a metal rod. The cylinder can be likened to a counterweight (an object chosen for its force of metaphor as it evokes both the lengthening of the nose mentioned in the title, and the telling of lies) or the clapper of a bell, the metal rod allowing for the swinging movement.[24] The sculpture is the first of a series of five propositions that all refer to Alberto Giacometti's *Le Nez*, as well as to two sculptures by Umberto Boccioni, *Development of a Bottle in Space* (1912) and *Unique Forms of Continuity in Space* (1913). For Rabinowitch, these works were suggestive of physical descriptions of movement mixing both operational methods and poetical formulations.[25] Giacometti created the first version of his sculpture (a head suspended on the inside of a frame composed of metal rods, out of which protrudes an unusually long nose) as early as 1947; however, the first bronze proofs were not cast until 1964, two years after Rabinowitch had begun work on his own series. Rabinowitch's sculpture is "abstract." The work has two colors: the oiled steel of the cone tends towards black, while the cylinder is brown. The piece rests upon the ground; its proportions are those of a person of average height. Moving around it, the observer notices, from the back and sides, an enclosed convex structure, and, from the front, an open, concave space within which there hangs an arrangement that recalls Giacometti's composition. The subtitle, *Central Order of Things and Events*, corresponds, according to Rabinowitch, to "Einstein's description of God."[26] The subtitle is chosen ironically in order to underline the rejection of the lie of illusionistic representation. The sculpture is conceived of as a sequence of operations: the rolling of the cone, and the hanging of the rod, leading the viewer to experience the time of the work's creation. Setting up the sculpture is an arduous process: first to be put in place is the heavy cylinder; the truncated cone is then set up around it as its chassis, and finally the cylinder is attached to the thin metal rod that keeps it at some distance from the ground. This work is the only one of the series that is in the MAMCO's collection. It is an arrangement capable of real movement, and it shows clearly its relations of fullness, emptiness, and mass. The cylinder also recalls *Universal Plumb Bob (Address to David Smith's "Five Units Equal")*, another series started in the same year.

Exhibition history

Rudiments d'un musée possible 1 – September 23, 1994–January 29, 1995
Rudiments d'un musée possible 2 – February 17, 1995–May 30, 1995
L'Éternel Détour – Summer sequence 2011 – Presentation of the collections 2011 (Summer) – June 8, 2011–September 18, 2011

Bibliography

Royden Rabinowitch, *Works 1962–1995*, Exh. cat., (Lodz: Muzeum Sztuki, 1995), pp. 51–57, ill. p. 57 #6.

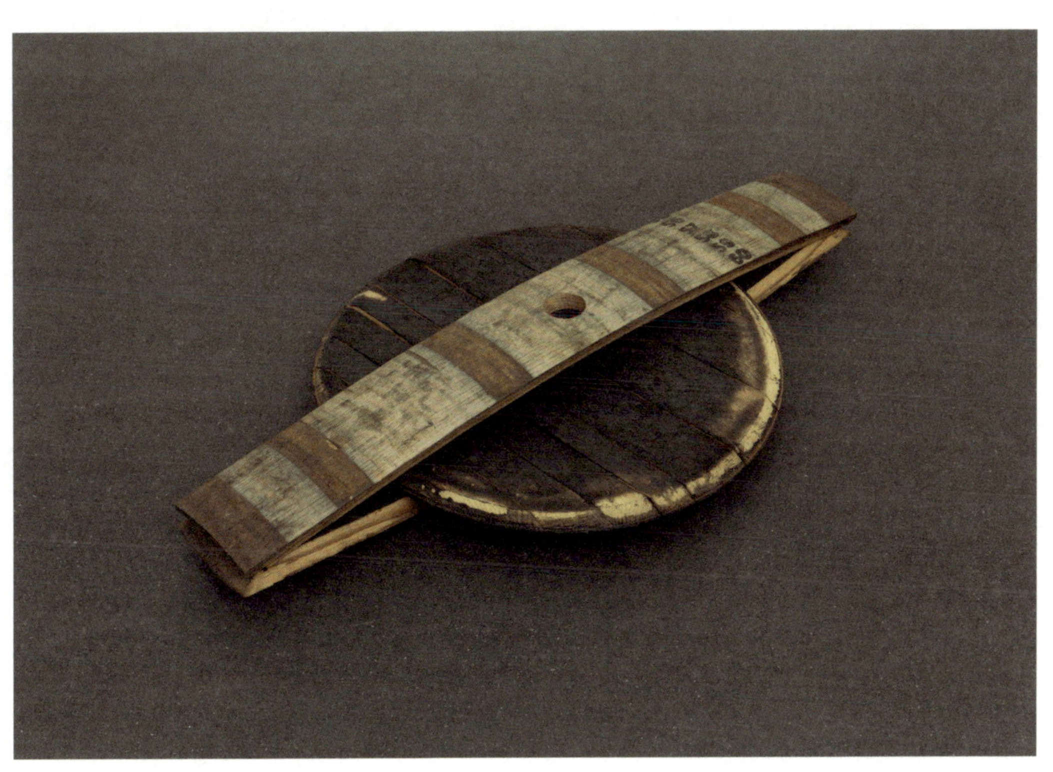

Barrel Construction (Double Curvature at Right Angles), 1963
Series: BARREL CONSTRUCTIONS—DOUBLE CURVATURES AT RIGHT ANGLES (CONSTRUCTION OF AN INTERNALLY DETERMINED NON-ANTHROPOMORPHIC NON-ARTICULATED BODY)
three-piece sculpture, oak barrel staves and head
10 × 89 × 53 cm (entire work)
MAMCO collection, gift of Max Wandeler
inv.: 2016–413 (1 to 3)

At ten years of age (1953), Rabinowitch is interested in the movement of a cement truck, embodying the rotation of a conic drum coupled with the translation of the cylindrical wheels:

> I compared the synthesis of this rotation and translation with the more unified synthesis of the wooden hooped barrel rolling along a single line. The hooped barrel of staves combined both zone and meridian methods of approximating spheres, i.e. conic sections (hoops) and cylindrical sections (staves) were used.[27]

In doing this, Rabinowitch breaks down and then reconstitutes pre-existing barrel parts,[28] integrating the barrel into his sculptures. He notes, "Considered the barrel one of the earliest embodiments of the newer culture, i.e. possessed great calculation and utility."[29] In this way, the artist sees the circles of the covers as defining latitudes, i.e. as zones, and the barrel staves as marking out longitudes, i.e. meridians. Here again, he notes, "Realized barrel was excellent model for double curvature (sphere/saddle constructed), i.e. with cylindrical and conic sections [...] (the barrel) was a perfect example of an implied infinity of directions in a construction."[30]

In *Barrel Construction (Double Curvature at Right Angles)*, Rabinowitch assembles, each one in opposition to the other, two staves, that encircle a partially charred barrel head. The side and bottom staves are oriented perpendicularly to one another, symbolizing geographical latitude and longitude. The pieces are held in equilibrium, one upon another, with no external means of assembly. He writes, "Regarding the burnt barrel parts: they were already burned. They are from used oak whiskey barrels which were purposely charred (which means partially burned to blacken the surface) to cure (flavor) the whiskey."[31]

Barrel Construction, begun in 1963, belongs to the canonical group of five sculptures that established the foundation of Rabinowitch's work at the beginning of the 1960s. Although the piece alludes to the human body (*Non-Articulated Body*), it avoids any anthropomorphic representation (*Non-Anthropomorphic*).[32]

In his analysis of Rabinowitch's "Barrel Constructions," Jan Hoet writes:

> His "Barrel Constructions" (1963/64) were produced at a moment when not only anthropomorphism was disappearing progressively from Western sculpture, but when even the so far unaffected doctrine of verticality, ultimately derived from a residue of anthropomorphism, began to be radically questioned."[33]

This might account, therefore, for the consistently horizontal development of the sculptures. These are among the smallest of Rabinowitch's sculptures; they concentrate the viewer's gaze on the details of the surface: "In fact it is just these properties of surface, color, material, which get magnified into details as size is reduced."[34]

Exhibition history

Rudiments d'un musée possible 1 – September 23, 1994–January 29, 1995
Rudiments d'un musée possible 2 – February 17, 1995–May 30, 1995
L'Éternel Détour – Summer sequence 2011 – Presentation of the collections 2011 (Summer) – June 8, 2011–September 18, 2011

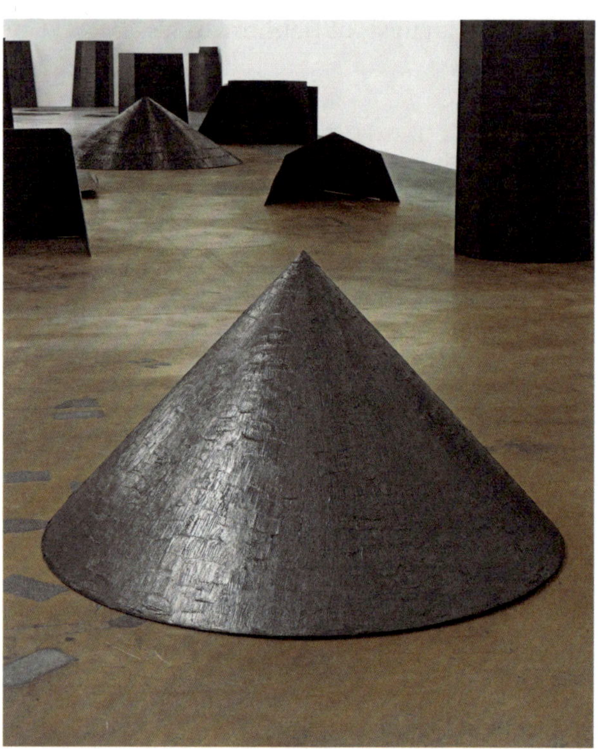

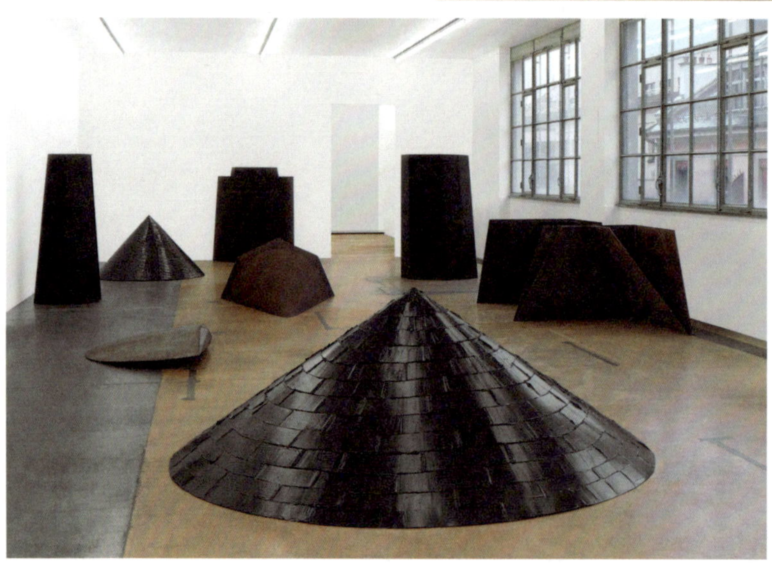

Discrete Green Vertically Greased Cone, 1965
Series: GREASED CONES (1ST CONSTRUCTION REGARDING INTERNAL CONDITIONS)
steel, grease
120 cm (height) × 168 cm (diameter)
MAMCO collection, gift of Max Wandeler
inv.: 2016–419

Dark Grey Horizontally Greased Cone, 1965
Series: GREASED CONES (1ST CONSTRUCTION REGARDING INTERNAL CONDITIONS)
steel, grease
105 (height) × 274 cm (diameter)
MAMCO collection, gift of Max Wandeler
inv.: 2016–429

These two sculptures are part of the series *Greased Cones*, the last of the five foundational works created by Rabinowitch between 1962 and 1965. In these foundational works, Rabinowitch was inspired by modernist sculpture and its abstract implifications. *Greased Cone* makes a reference to a drawing by Brancusi, *Portrait of James Joyce (1929–1930),* that appeared on the front cover of the book *Tales Told of Shem and Shaun: Three Fragments from Work in Progress* by Joyce.[35]

The *Greased Cones* (1965) are the result of a sequence of operations: the rolling of the cone, culminating in a construction that is hollow on the inside, and the greasing of the surface, a procedure that, since it cannot be carried out in an entirely even manner, makes the cone asymmetrical. The grease applied to the metal masks the subjacent material, and it changes the visual aspect of the sculpture. An opposition is set up between the static and industrial nature of the steel, and the amorphous and organic quality of the grease, the latter being spread thickly in successive horizontal circles, by means of a wide brush, either from the top to the base (*Dark Grey Horizontally Greased Cone*) or in random vertical strokes (*Discrete Green Vertically Greased Cone*). *Greased Cone* is a form that turns around upon itself, its surface offering us points of view that are equivalent, but that the irregular coating of grease prevents us from singling out. Despite the tactile quality of the surface, it is the visual experience of the sculpture that is foregrounded. The artist is interested in the limits of sculpture and of sculptural space. In adopting the form of its base, the grease in no way changes the general form of the sculpture, and the rigid base provides it with the structural support necessary to its characteristic organic chaos.

Beyond Rabinowitch's affinity with the work of Joseph Beuys, readily apparent in the pairing of metal and grease, the two artists' common interest in James Joyce was highlighted in the Belfast exhibition *Equilibrium? Royden Rabinowitch—Historical Turning Points and Artists' Solidarity*, in which Rabinowitch showed a greased cone.[36]

In 1993, Harald Szeemann invited Rabinowitch to participate with two of his *Greased Cones* in the exhibition *GAS (Grandiose, Ambitious, Silent)* that Szeemann was organizing at the CAPC in Bordeaux. "The grease covers only the surface of the cone, and it does not fill it. The surface is hidden, but its physical presence is recognizable. Due to its specific quality, the depth of the grease does not allow for an arbitrary increase in the size of the base. The greased cone is thus a possible marriage of the smooth metal and the stickiness capacity of the grease, the latter tending to liquify and flow—a metaphor of a conjunction of oppositions."[37]

The greased cone is perhaps the most emblematic of the artist's works. In February 2016, at Emergent in Belgium, Rabinowitch created a greased cone before a public audience, during a performance of his opera *Moby Dick or The Trouble with Physics*, accompanied on the violin by the Russian virtuoso Mikhail Bezverkhny. Behind the performers, a pendulum swung back and forth in front of two video projections, set up as a diptych, which showed sperm whales in their natural environment along with the rolling text of a passage from Herman Melville describing the whale's anatomy. In this particular context, the greased cone was suggestive of the snout of a submerged sperm whale.[38]

Dark Grey Horizontally Greased Cone has been shown at the MAMCO along with other works arranged in piles or evoking its conic form: César, *Le Sein* (1966); Reiner Ruthenbeck, *Weisser Papierhaufen* (1979); Hans Haacke, *Grass Grows* (1992).

Exhibition history

Discrete Green Vertically Greased Cone
Series: GREASED CONES (1ST CONSTRUCTION REGARDING INTERNAL CONDITIONS)
Vivement 2002! Sixth event – Presentation of the collections 2001 (Fall) – November 4, 2001–May 15, 2002
Rien ne presse / slow and steady / festina lente – First event – Presentation of the collections 2002 (Fall) – May 23, 2002–September 22, 2002
L'Éternel Détour – Summer sequence 2011 – Presentation of the collections 2011 (Summer) – June 8, 2011–September 18, 2011
Des histoires sans fin – Summer sequence 2015 – Presentation of the collections 2015 (Summer) – June 10, 2015–September 13, 2015
Récit d'un temps court – Presentation of the collections 2017 (Fall) – October 10, 2017–February 4, 2018

Bibliography

Royden Rabinowitch, *Works 1962–1995*, Exh. cat., (Lodz: Muzeum Sztuki, 1995), pp. 51–57, ill. p. 57 #6.
Rabinowitch, Sculpture 1962–1992, Exh. cat., (The Hague: Gemeentemuseum, 1992), ill. pp. 19–21 #3.

Exhibition history

Dark Grey Horizontally Greased Cone
Series: GREASED CONES (1ST CONSTRUCTION REGARDING INTERNAL CONDITIONS)

Rudiments d'un musée possible 1 – September 23, 1994–January 29, 1995
Rudiments d'un musée possible 2 – February 17, 1995–May 30, 1995
Patchwork in Progress 3 – Presentation of the collections 1998 (Fall) – July 1, 1998–October 11, 1998
Patchwork in Progress 7 et dernier – Presentation of the collections 1999 (Fall) – October 20, 1999–Dec. 23, 1999
Vivement 2002 ! First event – Presentation of the collections 2000 (Spring) – February 2, 2000–April 30, 2000
Vivement 2002 ! Second event – Presentation of the collections 2000 (Summer) – June 17, 2000–September 17, 2000
Vivement 2002 ! Third event – Presentation of the collections 2000 (Fall) – October 26, 2000–January 21, 2001
Vivement 2002 ! Fourth event – Presentation of the collections 2001 (Spring) – February 21, 2001–April 29, 2001
Vivement 2002 ! Fifth event – Presentation of the collections 2001 (Summer) – June 1, 2001–September 16, 2001
Vivement 2002 ! Sixth event – Presentation of the collections 2001 (Fall)– November 4, 2001–May 15, 2002
Rien ne presse / slow and steady / festina lente – First event – Presentation of the collections 2002 (Fall) – May 23, 2002–September 22, 2002.
L'Éternel Détour – Summer sequence 2011 – Presentation of the collections 2011 (Summer) – June 8, 2011–September 18, 2011

Bibliography

Royden Rabinowitch, *Works 1962–1995*, Exh. cat., (Lodz: Muzeum Sztuki, 1995), pp. 51–57, ill. p. 96 #35.

Hollow Panel, 1966
Series: HOLLOW PANELS (2ND CONSTRUCTION REGARDING INTERNAL CONDITIONS)
blued steel
31 × 30.5 cm
MAMCO collection, gift of Max Wandeler
inv.: 2016–430

Hollow Panel, 1966
Series: HOLLOW PANELS (2ND CONSTRUCTION REGARDING INTERNAL CONDITIONS)
blued steel
31 × 30.5 cm
MAMCO collection, gift of Max Wandeler
inv.: 2016–436

The *Hollow Panels* consist of two equal-sized rectangular plates, one on top of the other, with different thicknesses inserted along their borders, and with spaces between the varying thicknesses, these spaces pinched and the border sealed by a weld. On close examination an observer would be aware that this construction's interior could be either hollow or solid but that its front and back surfaces would always sustain a separation between themselves. [...] The knowledge that these constructions dealt with internal conditions, i.e. conditions obscured by surfaces, was based, I realized, on my experience with materials. I then generalized this realization thus: 'I know about internal conditions because of my experience with materials, my experience with materials is contingent upon my ability to act in space..."[39]

"These steel panels, standing out slightly from the wall, were created one year after the appearance of Donald Judd's article *Specific Objects*, and they can be seen as an examination, if not a critique, of Judd's position.[40] The adjective "hollow" indicates a depth, a negative relief, but it also signals something false, i.e. something sounds hollow, in the figurative sense. Should we see, *Hollow Panels*, as modular structures (often used in Minimalist art) that nonetheless, through their irregularity, undermine the Minimalist procedure?

These are the first of Rabinowitch's mural sculptures, and they were produced long before the later work, *Open Ice—For Gretzky*. The form here is the square; the edges are not linear, and, at regular intervals, there are signs of indentation and welding. The fine layer of blue-black iron oxide, covering the blued steel,[41] gives to the plates an uneven shine that focuses our attention on the unexpected surface effects. Each panel is individually attached to the wall. Jan Hoet has described them as being like manifestoes, declaring their desire for autonomy with regard to painting.[42]

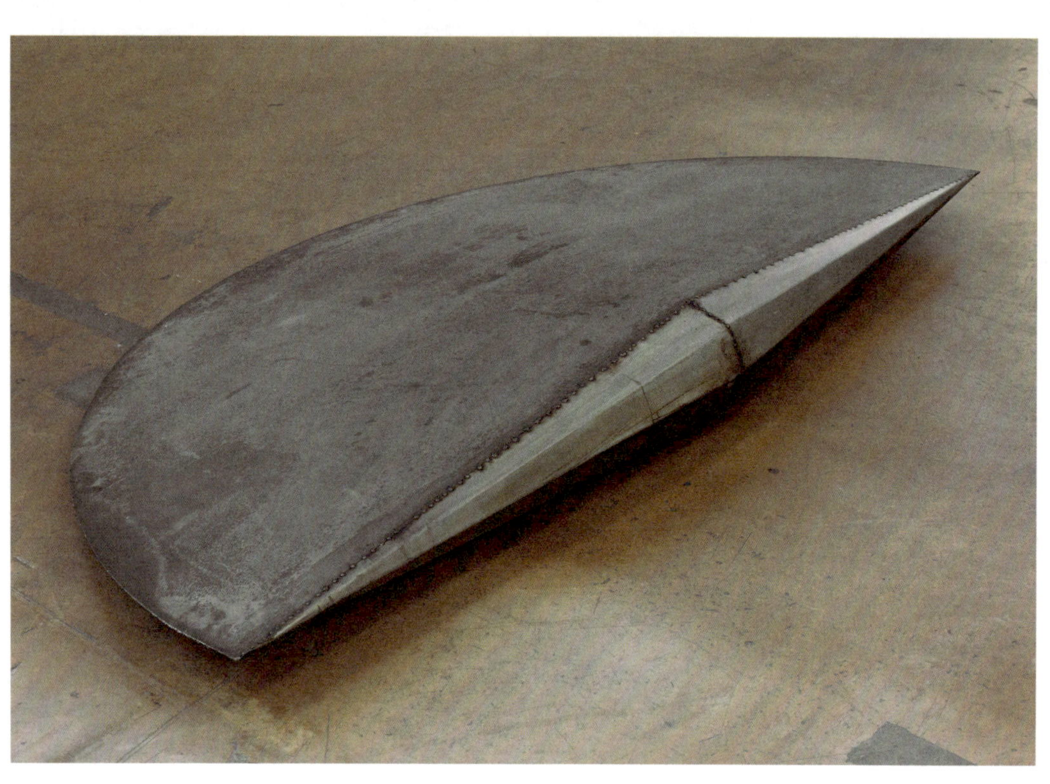

Conic Turnover, 1967
Series: CONIC TURNOVERS (3RD CONSTRUCTION REGARDING INTERNAL CONDITIONS)
cold-rolled steel
22 × 204.5 × 106.5 cm
MAMCO collection, gift of Max Wandeler
inv.: 2016–416

The sculpture lays on the ground. Its spatial configuration changes. As Rosalind Krauss has said of certain sculptures by David Smith, there is a "visual disjunction,"[43] i.e. the impossibility, despite the full and compact form of the sculpture, of our connecting together the various views of the work, and this is because there is no single privileged point of view. Horizontally symmetrical, the sculpture is composed of two, faceted half-cones connected together at their base, and extended, on top and below, by two rolled half-cones (laterally rolled conics) that fit perfectly with the increase in diameter of the cones to which they are welded. The rolled half-cones are attached along the entire length of the faceted half-cones, and the welding points are left visible. Arc-welding derives from David Smith who suggested, as early as 1947, that it be introduced into the teaching of the fine arts.[44] We should note, however, that Smith, as a former metal worker, belonged to the generation of artists who actually made their own sculptures, and this was not necessarily the case after the advent of Minimalist art. After his move to Europe in 1983, Rabinowitch has worked with a factory in Gent, where his sculptures are fabricated on the basis of his technical drawings and calculations for the production of developed or rolled surfaces. He takes part in the process of fabrication, and he is present, therefore, when the forms appear, circumventing sometimes his own predictions, which he considers a success. He likens the surprise that he feels at the sight of an unintended result to a victory over the idealism that he refutes in his work.[45] Certain of the works in this series, including this one, have the look of prototypes—the welds are less polished, and the more raw treatment of the surface is evidence of the artist's interest in the rendering of surfaces.

Exhibition history

Rudiments d'un musée possible 1 – September 23, 1994–January 29, 1995
Rudiments d'un musée possible 2 – February 17, 1995–May 30, 1995
L'Éternel Détour – Summer sequence 2011 – Presentation of the collections 2011 (Summer) – June 8, 2011–September 18, 2011
Récit d'un temps court – Presentation of the collections 2017 (Fall) – October 10, 2017–February 4, 2018.
Inventory – January 27, 2021–June 20, 2021

Bibliography

Royden Rabinowitch, *Works 1962–1995*, Exh. cat., (Lodz: Muzeum Sztuki, 1995), pp. 112–119, ill. p. 119 #52.

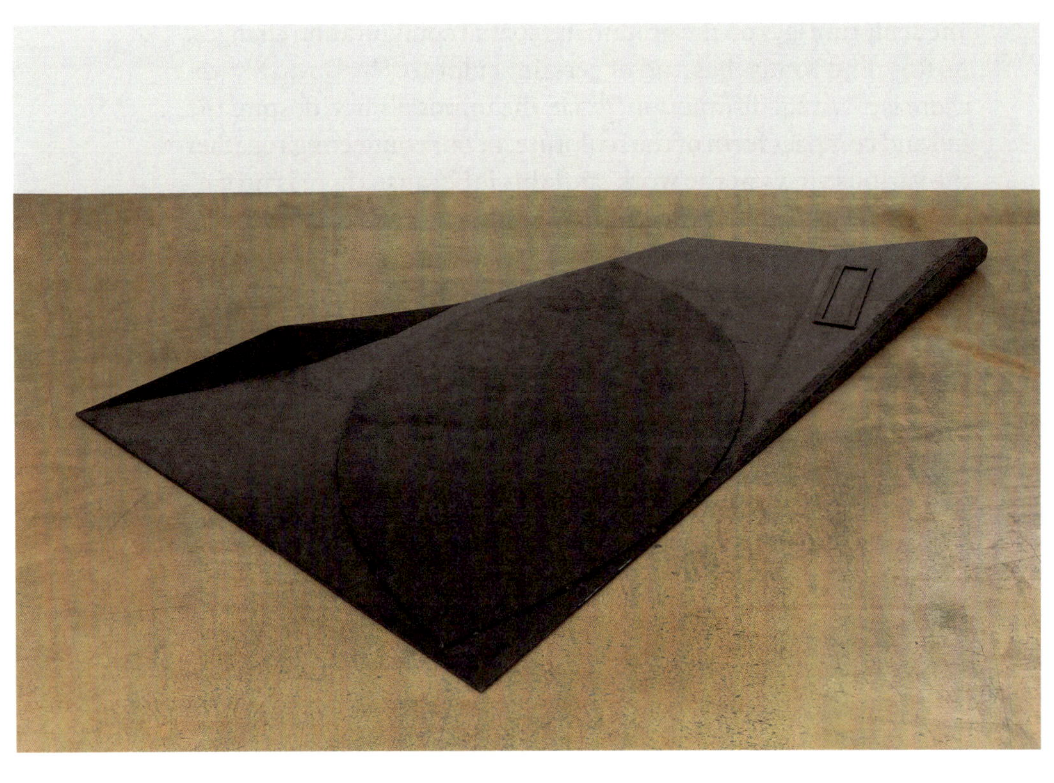

Karakorum (IV), 1968–1971
Series: KARAKORUM—SYNTHETIC CONSTRUCTION (SYNTHESIS OF PREVIOUS WORK)
oiled steel
7 × 162 × 290 cm
MAMCO collection, gift of Max Wandeler
inv.: 2016–422

Karakorum (IV) takes its name from the city of Karakorum, founded by Genghis Khan in his attempt to unite vanquished tribes prior to the attack on China. It is also the name of the highest road built by the Pakistani and Chinese armies, between 1966 and 1982, through the mountainous region in Kashmir that bears the same name—a highway that allows the traveler to cross peaks lying at an elevation of 4,693 meters.

Among Rabinowitch's works, this is a pivotal piece in which the artist creates a synthesis, within a single construction, of his prior work through a flattening, a stratification, a folding and welding together of previous forms.

> I had to make one construction so that, at a single glance, I could see objectively the implications behind all my previous work. [...] KARAKORUM was a kind of organic organization that seemed always to be located at some great distance like a strange, newly seen, distant city that somehow, from a different viewing point, might also hold the information for making a new body.[46]

The sculpture appears as if seen from a height, from a bird's eye view, and this has the effect of flattening out the volumes.

> I felt that I too had to synthesize or unite all the implications of the various constructions that I had previously made to have a chance at attacking a major sculptural assumption, i.e. the impossibility of making a fresh, i.e. more discrete, fully articulated body.[47]

Karakorum moves towards adopting the flatness of the ground, and, with the exception of two of its extremities, a vertical weld line, a riveted surround, and the layers that are added to it, its volume tends to disappear into the two-dimensionality of the plan; its constituent parts become almost graphic. Sculpture is here no longer necessarily something that one erects, as Rabinowitch had shown, in fact, as early as 1963, with his *Barrel Construction*, and as Carl Andre had made clear, the latter exploring horizontality with his arrangement of bricks at the exhibition *Primary Structures* in New York in 1966.[48] *Karakorum* prefigures the *Manifolds* (after 1972), a sequence of essentially flat sculptures that maintain, nonetheless, a connection with verticality, accentuating the *somatic* properties, i.e. what a conscious body feels as it moves about in space.

Exhibition history

Rudiments d'un musée possible 1 – September 23, 1994–January 29, 1995
Rudiments d'un musée possible 2 – February 17, 1995–May 30, 1995
L'Éternel Détour – Summer sequence 2011 – Presentation of the collections 2011 (Summer) – June 8, 2011–September 18, 2011
Récit d'un temps court – Presentation of the collections 2017 (Fall) – October 10, 2017–February 4, 2018

Bibliography

Royden Rabinowitch, *Works 1962–1995*, Exh. cat., (Lodz: Muzeum Sztuki, 1995), pp. 125–129, ill. p. 127 #55.
Rabinowitch, Sculpture 1962–1992, Exh. cat., (The Hague: Gemeentemuseum, 1992), pp. 135–137 #92.

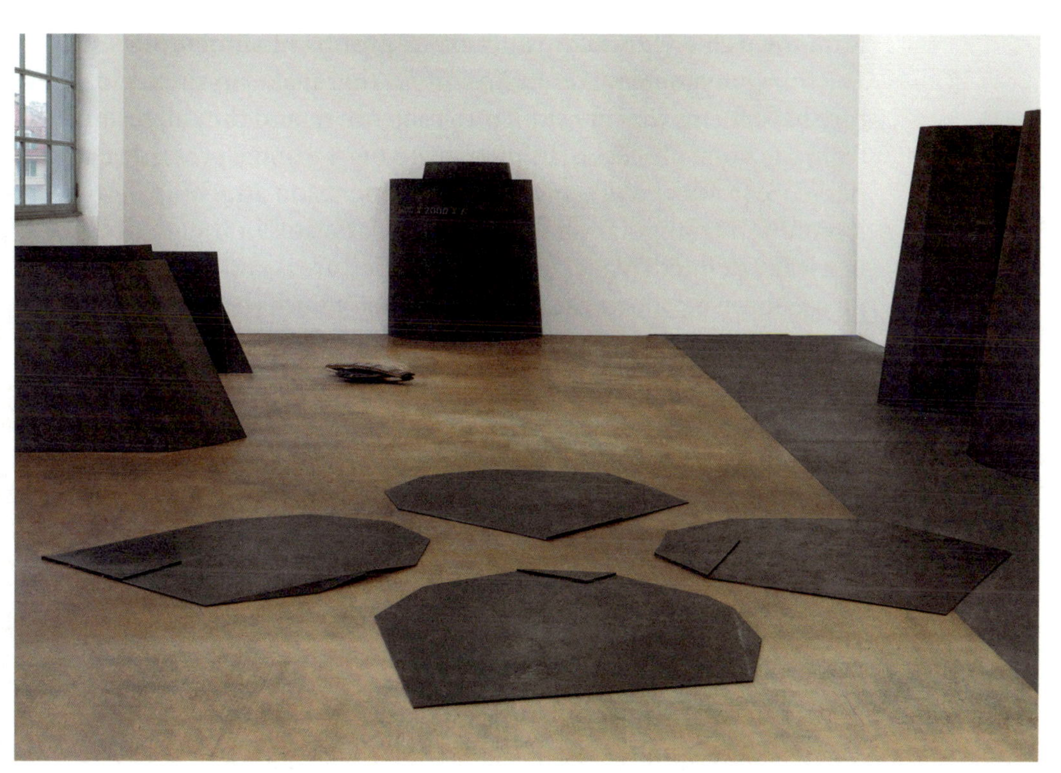

7 Manifolds in 4 Locations with Varied Handed Additions, 1986
Series: 2ND INTERNALLY DETERMINED FULLY ARTICULATED BODY (HANDED MANIFOLD GROUPS—GENERAL CASES OF HANDED DEVELOPED SURFACES OF ONE SIZE APPLIED TO PLANS) MAINTAINING LOCAL SOMATIC DESCRIPTIONS
four-piece sculpture, blackened and oiled steel
2 × [2.5 × 132.5 × 116 cm] / 2.5 × 130.5 × 115.5 cm / 2.5 × 130.7 × 118.5 cm
MAMCO collection, gift of Max Wandeler
inv.: 2016–423 (1 to 4)

Rabinowitch's *Manifolds* function as groups of similar pieces. The four polygonal plates (4 *Locations*) that make up the sculpture have forms that are similar to each other, and they all result from the same process of folding involving a manual press, seven per plate (7 *Manifolds*), and a welding operation attaching, horizontally, a triangular-shaped plate. A variation in the (mathematically defined) placement of the folded areas and the welded piece, however, allows the observer to distinguish them one from another. The facets are not flat, but have, rather, a slight incline. Each plate is lateralized, with the highest point from which the ribs either converge or move apart being placed to the right or left of the welded addition (*Varied Handed Additions*), focalizing thus the viewer's attention. As Jan Hoet describes it, "The folding operation actually transforms the plate into a very low, oblique, irregular and incomplete sided and faceted conic..."[49]

Thomas McEvilley, writing in the magazine *Artforum*, described the *Manifolds* as lying

> ...on the floor like large, irregularly folded papers, seeking neither to occupy our vision in the manner of freestanding sculpture nor, like so many works that hug the floor, to give an impression of massive weight.[50]

Along similar lines, Jan Hoet underscores the "hunger for 'floorness,'" that the *Manifolds* as a whole make apparent, and he cites Robert Pincus-Witten in this regard—the approach is a "concerted assault on the axiomatic verticality in sculpture" [51].

As with all of Rabinowitch's sculptures, the relation to the viewer and to space is at the heart of the arrangement. The differing orientations of the various plates affords the viewer, moving among and around them, the sense of an experience that repeats itself, or, as the artists puts it, "the experience of the same as different."

Exhibition history

Rudiments d'un musée possible 1 – September 23, 1994–January 29, 1995
Rudiments d'un musée possible 2 – February 17, 1995–May 30, 1995
Vivement 2002! Sixth event – Presentation of the collections 2001 (Fall) – November 4, 2001–May 15, 2002
Rien ne presse / slow and steady / festina lente – Water and Gas on all floors -- Third event – Presentation of the collections 2003 (Spring) – February 28, 2003–April 20, 2003
Mille et trois plateaux – 4th event – Number 2. Alfred Jensen, Royden Rabinowitch – October 25, 2005–January 15, 2006
Futur antérieur – L'Espèce de chose mélancolie – Presentation of the collections 2009 (Summer) – June 24, 2009–September 27, 2009
Futur antérieur – Le Principe d'incertitude – Presentation of the collections 2009 (Fall) – October 28, 2009–January 17, 2010
L'Éternel Détour – Summer sequence 2011 – Presentation of the collections 2011 (Summer) – June 8, 2011–September 18, 2011
Récit d'un temps court – Presentation of the collections 2017 (Fall) – October 10, 2017–February 4, 2018

Bibliography

Royden Rabinowitch, *Works 1962–1995*, Exh. cat., (Lodz: Musée Sztuki, 1995), pp. 144–151, ill. p. 151 #69.
Rabinowitch, Sculpture 1962–1992, Exh. cat., (The Hague: Gemeentemuseum, 1992), pp. 209–219 #130.

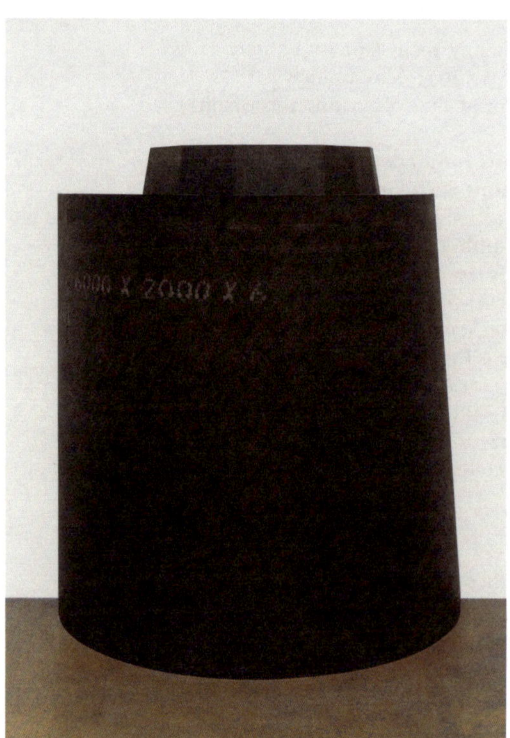

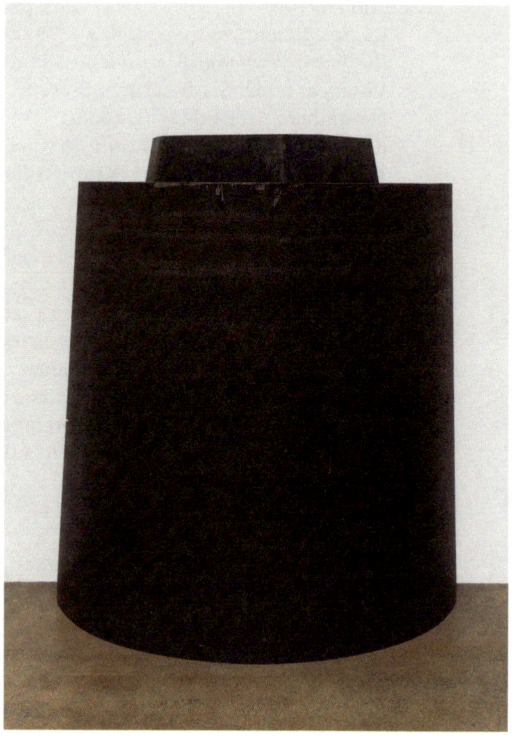

5th Lesson of Emanuel Feuermann (A), 1987
Series: 3RD INTERNALLY DETERMINED FULLY ARTICULATED BODY (LESSONS OF EMANUEL FEUERMANN—SPECIAL CASES OF HANDED DEVELOPED SURFACES OF TWO SIZES APPLIED TO AN ELEVATION MAINTAINING LOCAL SOMATIC DESCRIPTIONS)
two-piece sculpture, oiled steel
166.50 × 143 × 76 cm (entire work)
MAMCO collection, gift of Max Wandeler
inv.: 2016–414 (1 to 2)

5th Lesson of Emanuel Feuermann (B), 1987
Series: 3RD INTERNALLY DETERMINED FULLY ARTICULATED BODY (LESSONS OF EMANUEL FEUERMANN—SPECIAL CASES OF HANDED DEVELOPED SURFACES OF TWO SIZES APPLIED TO AN ELEVATION MAINTAINING LOCAL SOMATIC DESCRIPTIONS)
two-piece sculpture, oiled steel
168.5 × 153.5 × 77 cm (entire work)
MAMCO collection, gift of Max Wandeler
inv.: 2016–428 (1 to 2)

Begun in 1972, the *Manifolds* series, was to occupy Rabinowitch for more than ten years. After concluding this period of research, he went back to making upright developed sculptures[52] with his numbered series entitled, *Internally Determined Fully Articulated Body (Special Cases of Handed Developed Surfaces of Two Sizes Applied to a Plan and Elevation Maintaining Local Somatic Descriptions)*.

Since his childhood years, music has been a central part of Rabinowitch's life. He practiced the violin, and then studied the Greek foundations of music theory and the development of string and bow instruments at the University of Western Ontario School of Music, learning how the ways in which variations in the form of the instruments contributed to their sound. The cellist Emanuel Feuermann, to whom Rabinowitch dedicated a series of sculptures beginning in 1985, had a brief but dazzling career during which he revolutionized cello technique with his rare and inimitable instrument—a Stradivarius cello.[53] The *5th Lesson of Emanuel Feuermann...* includes two occurrences, (*A*) and (*B*), in oiled steel. They are similar in certain respects. Their constituent parts are half-volumes, with, in each case, the inner volume backing on to the wall. They both include a semi-circular part, enclosing a sided conic that is slightly more elevated. The curved surround of sculpture (*A*) has a deviation towards the right, whereas the deviation is towards the left in sculpture (*B*). Each sculpture, therefore, appears to be lateralized. The sides of the inner conics have different rhythms. They are narrower and more varied in (*A*), and wider and less numerous in (*B*).[54]

Exhibition history

Rudiments d'un musée possible 1 – September 23, 1994–January 29, 1995
Rudiments d'un musée possible 2 – February 17, 1995–May 30, 1995
Vivement 2002 ! Sixth event – Presentation of the collections 2001 (Fall) – November 4, 2001–May 15, 2002
L'Éternel Détour – Summer sequence 2011 – Presentation of the collections 2011 (Summer) – June 8, 2011–September 18, 2011
Récit d'un temps court – Presentation of the collections 2017 (Fall) – October 10, 2017–February 4, 2018

Bibliography

Royden Rabinowitch, *Works 1962–1995*, Exh. cat., (Lodz: Muzeum Sztuki, 1995), pp. 152–157, ill. p. 157 #72.
Rabinowitch, Sculpture 1962–1992, Exh. cat., (The Hague: Gemeentemuseum, 1992), pp. 221–229, no ill.

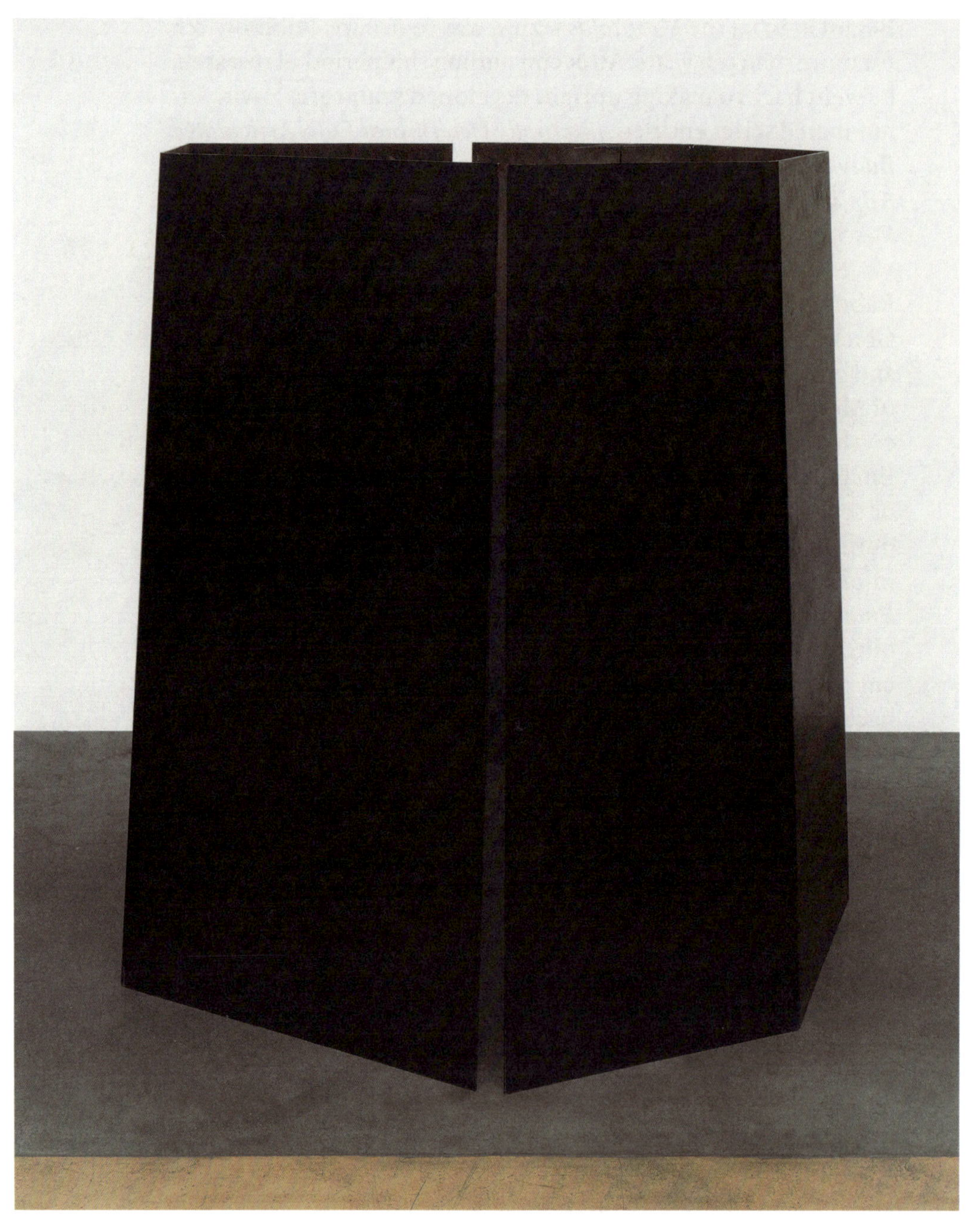

2nd of Two Opposed Developed Handed Surfaces Applied to Plans and Elevations Maintaining Local Somatic Descriptions, 1987–1988
Series: TWO OPPOSED DEVELOPED HANDED SURFACES (STARTED 1987) GENERAL CASE OF HANDED DEVELOPED SURFACES APPLIED TO PLANS AND ELEVATIONS MAINTAINING LOCAL SOMATIC DESCRIPTIONS
two-piece sculpture, rusted and oiled steel
150 × 150 × 151 cm (entire work)
MAMCO collection, gift of Max Wandeler
inv.: 2016–425 (1 to 2)

From this series on, the MAMCO's collection no longer includes any curved surfaces, although the forms of the surfaces do derive from the cone. The sculptures, each in two parts, are composed of steel plates that are more or less sided and symmetrical. The two parts face each other, making space for a slit, perpendicular to the wall, allowing the observer to perceive the internal space of the sculpture, to appreciate its mass, and to ascertain that the volume is not full. The final geometrical form, a polyhedron, results from the setting in equilibrium of the bended and opposed steel plates. Unlike Richard Serra's sculptures, these pieces are not monumental. They retain a human dimension, and they do not give rise to the sense of insecurity that one might feel as one moves alongside Serra's heavy walls of Corten steel.

Exhibition history

Rudiments d'un musée possible 1 – September 23, 1994–January 29, 1995
Rudiments d'un musée possible 2 – February 17, 1995–May 30, 1995
L'Éternel Détour – Summer sequence 2011 – Presentation of the collections 2011 (Summer) – June 8, 2011–September 18, 2011
Récit d'un temps court – Presentation of the collections 2017 (Fall) – October 10, 2017–February 4, 2018

Bibliography

Royden Rabinowitch, *Works 1962–1995*, Exh. cat., (Lodz: Muzeum Sztuki, 1995), pp. 165–167, ill. #72.
Rabinowitch, Sculpture 1962–1992, Exh. cat., (The Hague: Gemeentemuseum, 1992), pp. 237–239, ill. pp. 237–239 #136.

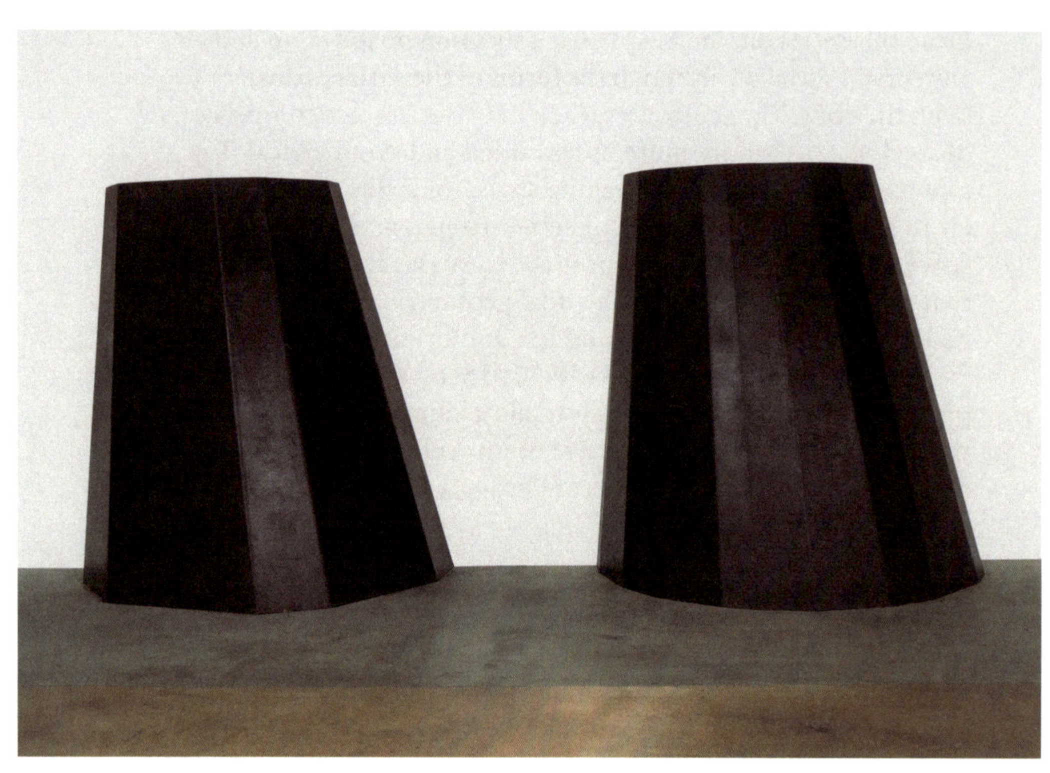

Disposition of an Internally Determined Fully Articulated Body (1st General Case of Handed Developed Surfaces of One Size Applied to Plans and Elevations Maintaining Local Somatic Descriptions), 1988
Series: DISPOSITION OF AN INTERNALLY DETERMINED FULLY ARTICULATED BODY (SINGULAR, SPECIAL, AND GENERAL CASES OF HANDED DEVELOPED SURFACES OF ONE SIZE APPLIED TO PLANS AND ELEVATIONS MAINTAINING LOCAL SOMATIC DESCRIPTIONS)
two-piece sculpture, oiled steel
184.5 × 180 × 102 cm / 184.5 × 182.5 × 102 cm
MAMCO collection, gift of Max Wandeler
inv.: 2016–424 (1 to 2) inv.: 2016–424 (1 à 2)

The arrangement is the same as with the *Homages to Emanuel Feuermann*. The single block pieces are backing onto the wall, yet they appear to have been placed indifferently, side by side (MAMCO) or diametrically opposite one another (Lodz). The surfaces are faceted differently. The oiled steel treatment gives them a coppered hue such as might be likened to a hammered bronze, where the surfaces catch the light at varying angles. The pieces are of exactly the same size, and they lean at the same inclination, perhaps like classical dancers at rest. Rudi Fuchs, in fact, has no qualms about using this comparison with some of Rabinowitch's sculptures:

There is, however, a curious parallel in the small bronze figures of dancers by Degas. In studying impossibly precarious movement, Degas observed the ballet—making those beautiful and tender figures which actually show movements carried to their physical limit where the posture is maintained at the strenuous point of near collapse. Something similar I sense in the work of Royden Rabinowitch: a similar concern with the careful development of shaped surfaces, leading them to the most surprising definitions where then they somehow remain, unbelievingly light like the dancer balancing on her toes.[55]

Exhibition history

Rudiments d'un musée possible 1 – September 23, 1994– January 29, 1995
Rudiments d'un musée possible 2 – February 17, 1995–May 30, 1995
Futur antérieur - Le Principe d'incertitude – Presentation of the collections 2009 (Fall) – October 28, 2009–January 17, 2010
L'Éternel Détour – Summer sequence 2011 – Presentation of the collections 2011 (Summer) – June 8, 2011–September 18, 2011
Récit d'un temps court – Presentation of the collections 2017 (Fall) – October 10, 2017–February 4, 2018

Bibliography

Royden Rabinowitch, *Works 1962–1995*, Exh. cat., (Lodz: Muzeum Sztuki, 1995), pp. 168–181, ill. p.179 #77.

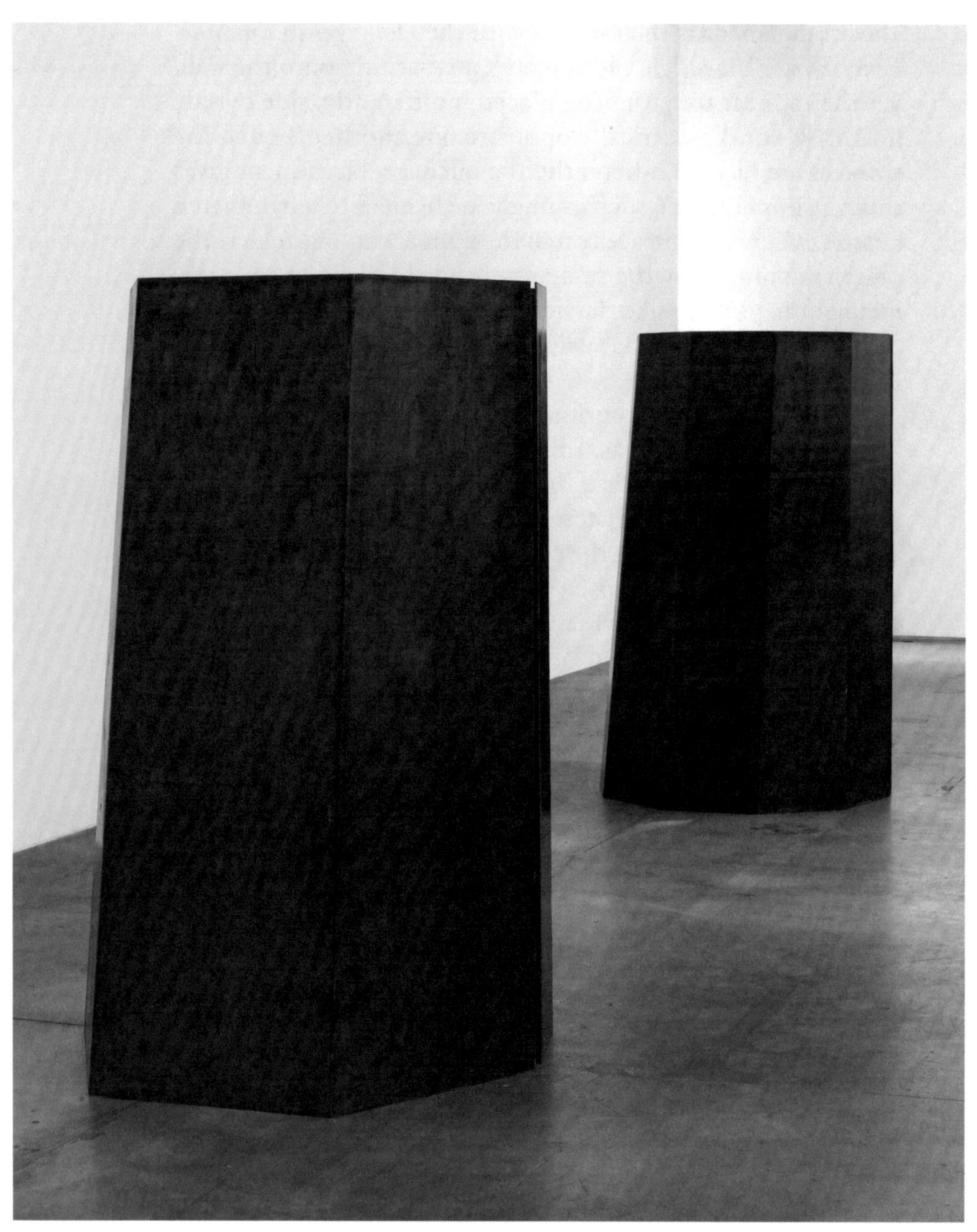

1st of Six Opposed Handed Developed Same-Sized Surfaces, 1989
(General Case of Opposed Handed Developed Same-Sized Surfaces Applied to Plans and Elevations Maintaining Local Somatic Descriptions—Axes Perpendicular to Wall)
Series: SINGULAR, SPECIAL AND GENERAL CASES OF OPPOSED HANDED DEVELOPED SAME-SIZED SURFACES APPLIED TO PLANS AND ELEVATIONS MAINTAINING LOCAL AND SOMATIC DESCRIPTIONS ORGANIZED REGARDING DIAMETERS AND/ OR AXES (STARTED 1987)
six-piece sculpture, blued and oiled steel
182.5 × 122 × 113 cm (each piece)
MAMCO collection, gift of Max Wandeler
inv.: 2016–415 (1 to 6)

As indicated in the second part of the title, these sculptures have their axes perpendicular to the wall. The two panels of each of the six pieces have identical surface areas, but they are faceted and inclined differently, one to the right, and the other to the left. Presented one opposite the other, the inner space of the panels is hollow. Each piece is composed of two faceted metal surfaces, bent with a hand press, but the volume of each pair as a whole is that of a polyhedron. The pieces are on a human scale, and they have a rhythm provided by the slight inclination of each piece to the right or left, a revival of the *contrapposto* characteristic of the Greek statues of Polycleites—a suggested anthropomorphism, therefore, with which the observer can identify.

Exhibition history

Rudiments d'un musée possible 1 – September 23, 1994–January 29, 1995
Rudiments d'un musée possible 2 – February 17, 1995–May 30, 1995
L'Éternel Détour – Summer sequence 2011 – Presentation of the collections 2011 (Summer) – June 8, 2011–September 18, 2011
Récit d'un temps court – Presentation of the collections 2017 (Fall) – October 10, 2017–February 4, 2018

Bibliography

Royden Rabinowitch, *Works 1962–1995*, Exh. cat., (Lodz: Muzeum Sztuki, 1995), p. 181, ill. #77.
Rabinowitch, Sculpture 1962–1992, Exh. cat., (The Hague: Gemeentemuseum, 1992), pp. 240–257, ill. pp. 250–253 #140.

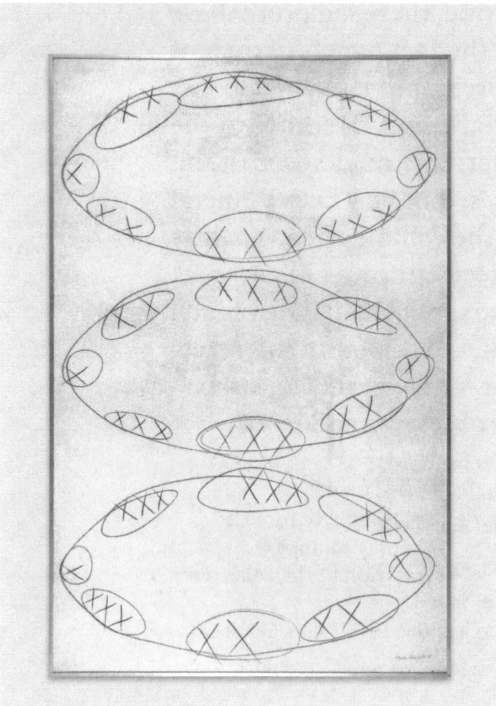

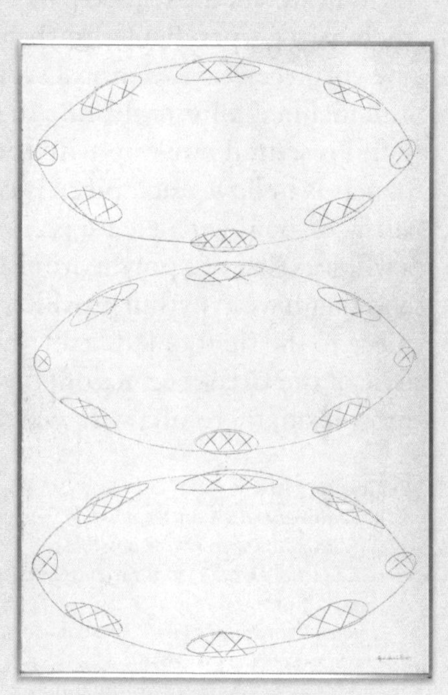

Singular Case of Handed Operator Bundles Through Two Axes Limited to Local Ocular Descriptions ("Who Ordered This?"), 1990
Series: *GUIDES TO THE VERTICAL PLAN OF ORDINARY EXPERIENCE (SINGULAR AND COLOURED CASES OF HANDED OPERATOR BUNDLES THROUGH TWO AXES LIMITED TO LOCAL OCULAR DESCRIPTIONS)*
graphite on prepared canvas
300 × 200 cm (framed)
MAMCO collection, gift of Max Wandeler
inv.: 2016–410 and 2016–411

For someone such as Rabinowitch, the practice of drawing is more than a technique of visual representation on a flat support. It is a case of bringing to bear Monge's descriptive geometry and Poincaré's ordinary space of experience; it involves thinking about objects as if they were situated within geometrical space; it means confronting science and what is intelligible with art and the unintelligible; and it entails localizing an object by picturing to oneself the movements necessary in order to reach the object. Rabinowitch produced the first drawings of his sculptures in 1974, after having created the *Handed Manifold*, his first somatic construction. He was exploring the possibilities of creating a somatic drawing, in other words, of translating into two dimensions a three-dimensional artwork.[56]

These two pieces were created for the exhibition of drawings *Who Ordered This?*, directed by Jan Hoet in 1990 on La Gomera (Canary Islands). Rabinowitch produced the works on the site.

> I did the drawings in the exhibition space at night listening to the ocean outside wash back and forth over the wonderfully smooth stones composing the beach which, undoubtedly, influenced my treatment of the plane, the size of which was determined by the extent of my reach.[57] These freely connected points of major ellipses developing approximations of minor ellipses marked differently are my acknowledgment to myself that standing still rules out the possibility of any synthesis at all. *Who Ordered This? is a quote of one of my distant relatives* Isador Isaac Rabi (a noble prize winner in physics) who reportedly blurted this out when he was confronted with a proposal in physics that stopped him from moving towards a physical synthesis. A drawing only makes sense to me when I stand still and only my eyes move.[58]

Recalling how he had been struck by the internal organization, culminating in an extraordinary immobility, of the sculpted figures of the tombs of the Dukes of Burgundy, Rabinowitch set down and tested out a working method involving movement of his eyes, closing of his eyes, comparing this movement with the bending of flat surfaces in the production of his sculptures, and rediscovering the memory of space when the body was in movement.[59] Once finished, the artist had these large drawings framed in Plexiglass. He did so, as he explains it, "so as to remove any emphasis on material I completed the drawing by covering it with plexiglass which reflected light and cut off observers from the material..."[60]—a frame, therefore, to differentiate the space of the drawing from the surrounding space.

Exhibition History

Who Ordered This?: drawings 1990, La Gomera, Atelier del Sur, Canaries Islands – October 27, 1990–December 29, 1990 (exhibition organized by Jan Hoet)
Rudiments d'un musée possible 1 – September 23, 1994–January 29, 1995
Rudiments d'un musée possible 2 – February 17, 1995–May 30, 1995
Futur antérieur – L'Espèce de chose mélancolie – Presentation of the collections 2009 (Summer) – June 24, 2009–September 27, 2009

Bibliography

Royden Rabinowitch—Who Ordered This?, Exh. cat., (La Gomera, Canary Islands: Atelier del Sur), n. p. (Jan Hoet interview with the artist).

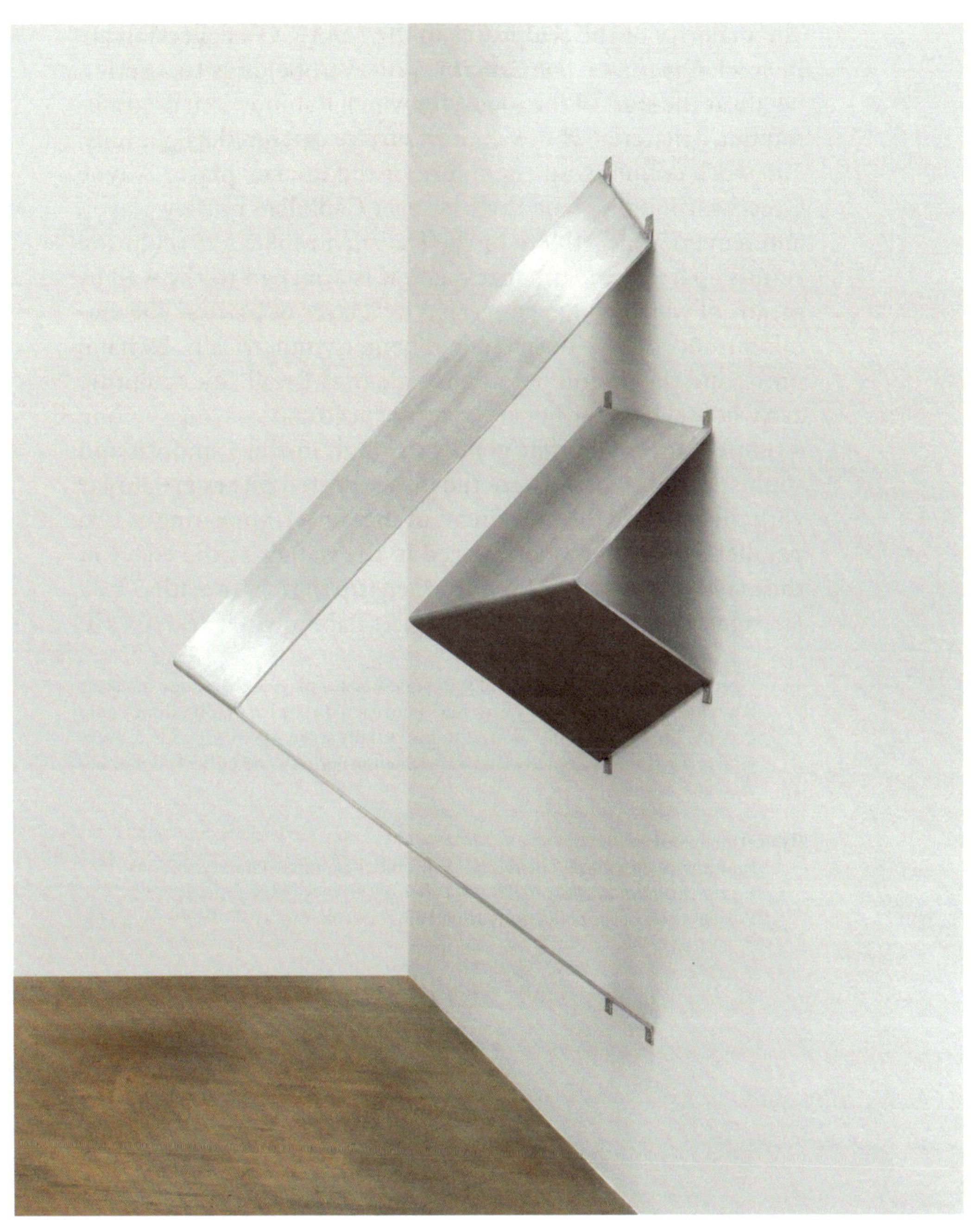

Open Ice—For Gretzky, 1991
(SINGULAR CASES OF HANDED DEVELOPED SURFACES OF TWO SIZES APPLIED TO THE LIMIT OF THE ELEVATION MAINTAINING LOCAL SOMATIC DESCRIPTIONS)
two-piece sculpture, aluminum
214 × 92 × 107 cm (entire work)
MAMCO collection, gift of Max Wandeler
inv.: 2016–412 (1 to 2)

The majority of the sculptures in the MAMCO's collection are in steel. *Open Ice—For Gretzky*, however, belongs to a series, begun at the start of the 1990s, for which Rabinowitch used aluminum, a material whose smooth surface catches the light fully. The work conjures up the figure of the hockey player Wayne Gretzky, thought to be the best ever Canadian hockey player, and named Male Athlete of the Decade in 1989. The sculpture stands apart in one other respect: it is attached to the wall by means of wall anchors concealed by a layer of plaster. The aluminum sheets have been cut and bent asymmetrically, by hand press, and they stand out at an angle to the wall. The sculpture as a whole evokes the hockey player's speed and swaying rhythm: a refined approach that comes through in this "smooth and sophisticated" work, where the disconnected pieces are at play with the wall and the movement of the viewer, appearing as two parallel half-lozenges ensconced in the wall or as the edges of the player's skates as he literally opens up the ice. The title, *Open Ice*, refers to Gretzky's style of play. As Rabinowitch describes it:

> *Open Ice* was used by the world's greatest hockey player to describe his basic strategy. His whole effort was to find a position on the ice that he alone could occupy, thus positioning himself to potentially score a goal. Of course, every vital artist thinks in exactly this way, which is perhaps the only thinking that vital artists share.[61]

Exhibition history

Rudiments d'un musée possible 1 – September 23, 1994–January 29, 1995
Rudiments d'un musée possible 2 – February 17, 1995–May 30, 1995
Presentation of the collections 2018 (Fall) – October 10, 2018–February 3, 2019

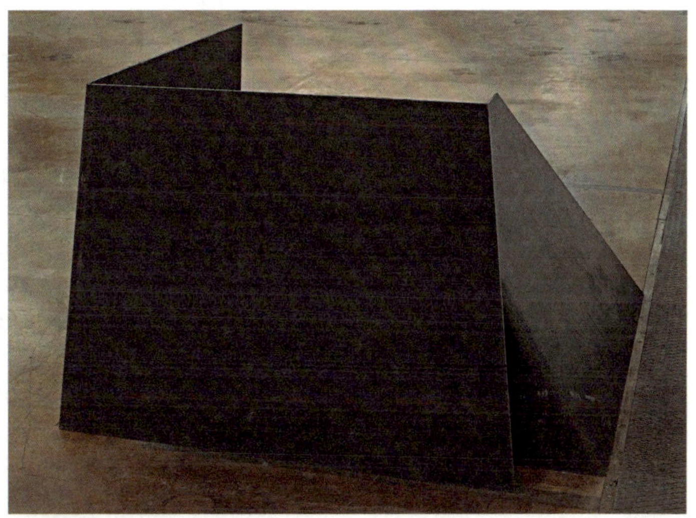
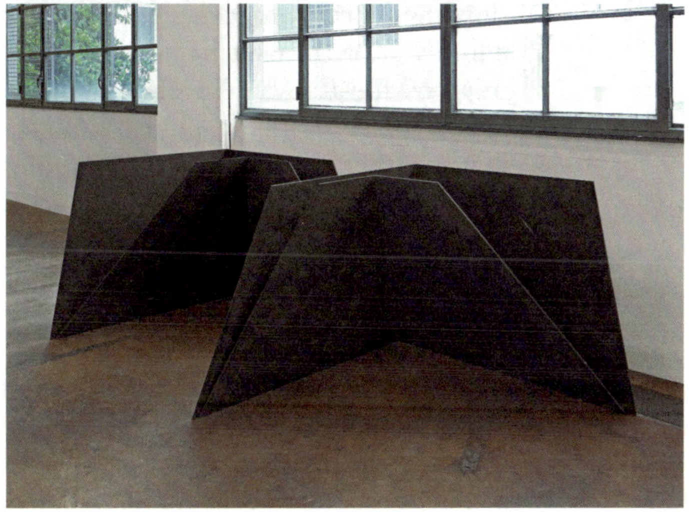

Double Clutching (for John Coltrane), 1991
Special Case of Handed Developed Surfaces of 2 Sizes Applied to a Plan and Elevation Maintaining Local Somatic Descriptions
Series: DISPOSITION OF AN INTERNALLY DETERMINED FULLY ARTICULATED BODY (SINGULAR, SPECIAL AND GENERAL CASES OF HANDED DEVELOPED SURFACES OF TWO SIZES APPLIED TO PLANS AND/OR ELEVATIONS MAINTAINING LOCAL SOMATIC DESCRIPTIONS)
two-piece sculpture, oiled steel
92 × 126 × 126 cm (uppermost piece) / 76 × 125 × 125 cm (lowermost piece)
MAMCO collection, gift of Max Wandeler
inv.: 2016–427 (1 to 2)

Double Clutching—After Cecil Taylor, 1991
(Singular Case of Handed Developed Surfaces of Two Sizes Applied to a Plan and Elevation Maintaining Local Somatic Descriptions)
Series: DISPOSITIONS OF AN INTERNALLY DETERMINED FULLY ARTICULATED BODY (SINGULAR, SPECIAL AND GENERAL CASES OF HANDED SURFACES OF TWO SIZES APPLIED TO PLANS AND/OR ELEVATIONS MAINTAINING LOCAL SOMATIC DESCRIPTIONS)
four-piece sculpture, rusted and oiled steel
105 × 142 × 141 cm / 101.5 × 141 × 143 cm (uppermost pieces)
101 × 139 × 139 cm / 101 × 139 × 139 cm (lowermost pieces)
MAMCO collection, gift of Max Wandeler
inv.: 2016–418 (1 to 4)

Double Clutching—After Cecil Taylor is a four-piece sculpture set out in two pairs. The first pairing includes an outer sheet, bent vertically so as to create two facets of unequal length (a large and a small side), both of which are inclining towards the inside, and the ends of which are cut at an angle to the perpendicular. The inside of this sheet is doubled by another metal plate that appears to be of about the same height. This inner plate is also bent vertically, with the bend placed along the short side of the outer sheet of metal. Its sides are cut at an oblique angle, with the lower part of each side lining up with the bottom of the corresponding facet of the outer sheet. In the second pairing, this configuration is repeated, with, however, one variation: this time the bend in the inner sheet is placed against the longer side of the outer plate. This gives a different orientation to each pairing, suggesting possibly the repetitive accents of syncopated rhythms along with improvisation freed from traditional conventions—Cecil Taylor's *free jazz*. The sculpture involves a "clutching" of two apparently identical and yet unique pieces. This is not the repetition of the same, neither is it Carl Andre's *One thing after another*.

Double Clutching (for John Coltrane) belongs to the same series as the preceding work, and it relates to the more well-known avant-garde jazz figure, John Coltrane. Here again, the piece is composed of two metal sheets of varying heights. The taller outer sheet, with two facets leaning toward the inside, unequal in length and cut at an angle at the sides, is paired with another L-shaped sheet, its sides more angled, and also cut at an oblique angle. The inner piece is set at right angles to the enveloping sheet. The bending of the metal sheets, each of which measures one half centimeter in thickness (the typical thickness of the metal used by Rabinowitch), has the effect of moving them from plane to volume. The two sculptures are developments of the *Handed Manifold Group*.

Exhibition history

Rudiments d'un musée possible 1 – September 23, 1994–January 29, 1995
Rudiments d'un musée possible 2 – February 17, 1995–May 30, 1995
L'Éternel Détour – Summer sequence 2011 – Presentation of the collections 2011 (Summer) – June 8, 2011–September 18, 2011
Récit d'un temps court – Presentation of the collections 2017 (Fall) – October 10, 2017–February 4, 2018

Bibliography

Royden Rabinowitch, *Works 1962–1995*, Exh. cat., (Lodz: Muzeum Sztuki, 1995), pp. 182–203, no ill.
Rabinowitch, Sculpture 1962–1992, Exh. cat., (The Hague: Gemeentemuseum, 1992), pp. 299–303, no ill.

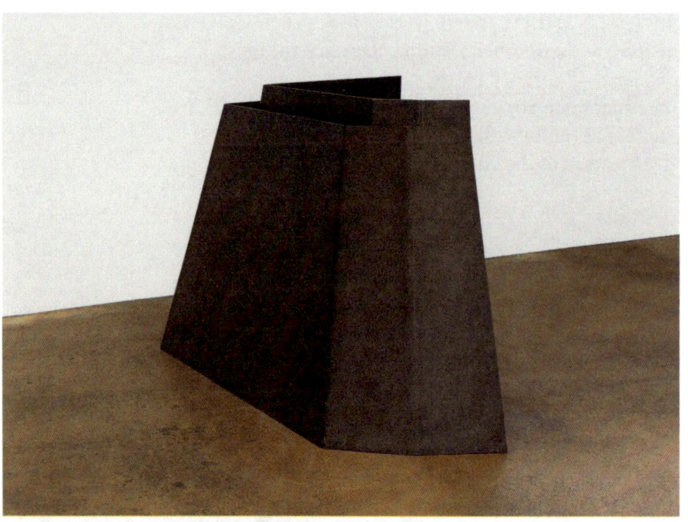

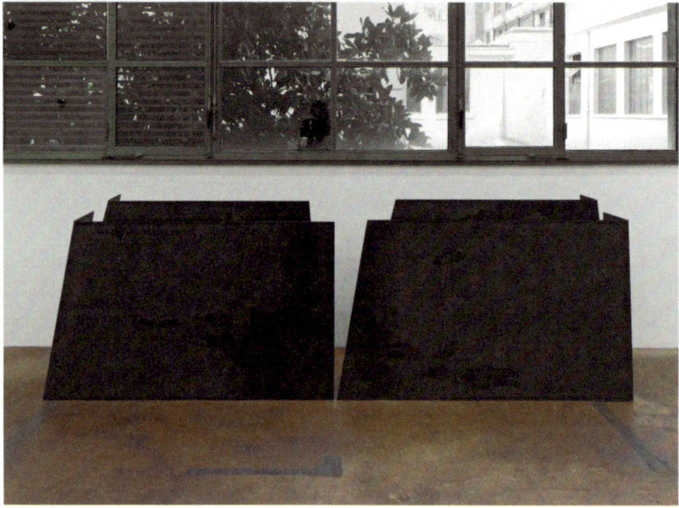

1st Special Case B of Handed Operator Bundles Through Three Axes Limited to Local Somatic Descriptions (Length Perpendicular to Wall), 1993
Series: GUIDES TO THE FULL SPACE OF ORDINARY EXPERIENCE (SPECIAL AND GENERAL CASES OF HANDED OPERATOR BUNDLES THROUGH THREE AXES LIMITED TO LOCAL SOMATIC DESCRIPTIONS)
two-piece sculpture, steel
107 × 156.50 × 106 cm (uppermost piece) / 98.50 × 204 × 122 cm (lowermost piece)
MAMCO collection, gift of Max Wandeler
inv.: 2016–426 (1 to 2)

1st Special Case C of Handed Operator Bundles Through Three Axes Limited to Local Somatic Descriptions (Length Parallel to Wall), 1993
Series: GUIDES TO THE FULL SPACE OF ORDINARY EXPERIENCE (SPECIAL AND GENERAL CASES OF HANDED OPERATOR BUNDLES THROUGH THREE AXES LIMITED TO LOCAL SOMATIC DESCRIPTIONS PARALLEL TO WALL)
four-piece sculpture, oiled steel
101.5 × 137.5 × 35.5 cm (uppermost pieces) / 91 × 148 × 39 cm (lowermost pieces)
MAMCO collection, gift of Max Wandeler
inv.: 2016–421 (1 to 4)

For Rabinowitch, these sculptures are developments of the *Handed Manifold Group*, the latter reinforcing the message of the *Handed Manifold*. Whereas the *Handed Manifold* applies itself to a momentary description of space, the *Handed Manifold Group* consists of an accumulation of momentary descriptions. These descriptions delineate the range, in elevation, of the description of a full space according to three axes: vertical, horizontal, and oblique. The sculptures here are pairings whose twin component parts are worked differently in terms of height and treatment of the inner and outer sheets. Their modest height scarcely surpasses one meter. Their placement, perpendicular to the wall (*Special Case B*) or parallel to it (*Special Case C*), determines whether or not the viewer has access to the internal face of the sculptures. As is made clear in the Lodz exhibition catalogue, the variety of forms of this series appears to be infinite, and this is true even if, as we have stressed, the generic forms remain the cylinder and cone. As Rabinowitch explains it:

> There is an unlimited number of concrete models of any local/somatic operator [...]. But there is only one concrete model of any strictly rational/empirical operator (a cone within a cylinder of the same base and height – the cylinder, the analogue of the invariants or principles of any physical theory; the cone, the analogue of the variables or observations verifying or falsifying any physical theory).[62]

Exhibition history

Rudiments d'un musée possible 1 – September 23, 1994–January 29, 1995
Rudiments d'un musée possible 2 – February 17, 1995–May 30, 1995
Récit d'un temps court – Presentation of the collections 2017 (Fall) – October 10, 2017–February 4, 2018

Bibliography

Royden Rabinowitch, *Works 1962–1995*, Exh. cat., (Lodz: Muzeum Sztuki, 1995), pp. 207–331, ill. pp. 224–229 #90.
Royden Rabinowitch, *Works 1962–1995*, Exh. cat., (Lodz: Muzeum Sztuki, 1995), pp. 207–331, ill. pp. 222–223 #89.

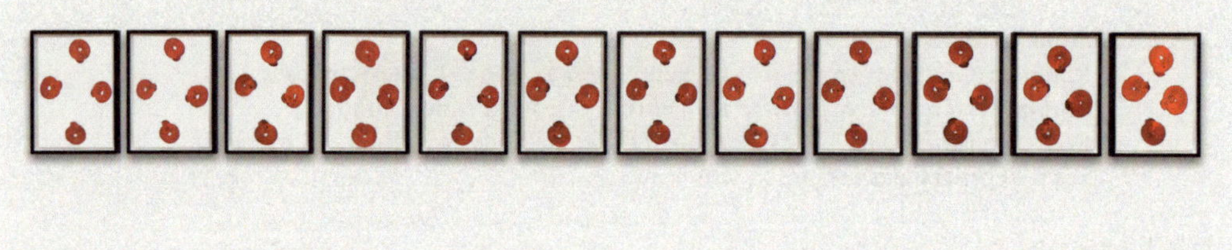

Coloured Case of Handed Operator Bundles Through Two Axes Limited to Local Ocular Descriptions, 1993
Series: GUIDES TO THE VERTICAL PLAN OF ORDINARY EXPERIENCE—COLOURED CASES OF HANDED OPERATOR BUNDLES THROUGH TWO AXES LIMITED TO LOCAL OCULAR DESCRIPTIONS
acrylic on linen canvas
300 × 200 cm
MAMCO collection, gift of Max Wandeler
inv.: 2016–408 et 2016–409

Judgment on Freedom and Necessity, 1996
set of 12 watercolors on drawing paper
42 × 29.2 cm (each piece unframed)
MAMCO collection, gift of Christian Bernard
inv.: 1996–493 (1 to 12)

Rabinowitch considers drawing to be a "collection of events" bearing upon the examination of three basic elements: sculpture, space, and the viewer, all of them brought to a two-dimensional plane on large-size canvases or small sheets of drawing paper, and emphasizing, in particular, the viewer's perceptual capacities. His titles are, for the artist, poetic creations, and they appear to arise from a protocol established by an empirical experimenter; namely, the viewer, who establishes the topography of the space of the work, takes the measure of the work's various sides and surfaces, increasing the number of points of view in order to gauge its contour, mass, folds, empty spaces, and its relation to verticality and horizontality.

Judgment on Freedom and Necessity, 1996, is an allusion to the great essay by the philosopher and ethicist Alfred Jules Ayer, and to the insoluble problem of moral responsibility. As Rabinowitch puts it:

> *Freedom and Necessity* places before all readers one of the major aspects of the irresolvable friction between any direct observer (any local/somatic operator) and any consensual norm (any rational/empirical operator), an aspect moreover that is at the center of my internal struggle with idealism which, as an artist, ironically enough, is expressed interpersonally and with considerably more irony, only in terms of judgments on impersonal matters.[63]

Each canvas or sheet of drawing paper is a space occupied by four motifs set out in two mirrored pairs. Each of the motifs represents a circle, extended by an appendage—a turning, materialized by an abstract schematic, around an imaginary point. Roman Kurzmeyer describes it thus: "The artist has visualized four uniform movements or articulations of his painting hand. He describes the four figures as mirrored on two axes (horizontal and vertical). Despite this conceptual clarity and methodological rigour, four individual particular forms result..."[64] The signs take up the cardinal points of the canvas, and it is as if they are held at a distance from one another by a centrifugal force. The canvas is in portrait format, large enough to encompass the whole of the artist's body, and the mirrored motifs are positioned equidistantly from the edges. The two large paintings and the twelve small drawings are in color, and they prompt thoughts on Goethe's theory of colors, the only thing, according to Rabinowitch, that cannot be integrated into a theory in physics.[65]

Exhibition history

Rudiments d'un musée possible 1 – September 23, 1994–January 29, 1995
Rudiments d'un musée possible 2 – February 17, 1995–May 30, 1995
L'Éternel Détour – Summer sequence 2011 – Presentation of the collections 2011 (Summer) – June 8, 2011– September 18, 2011

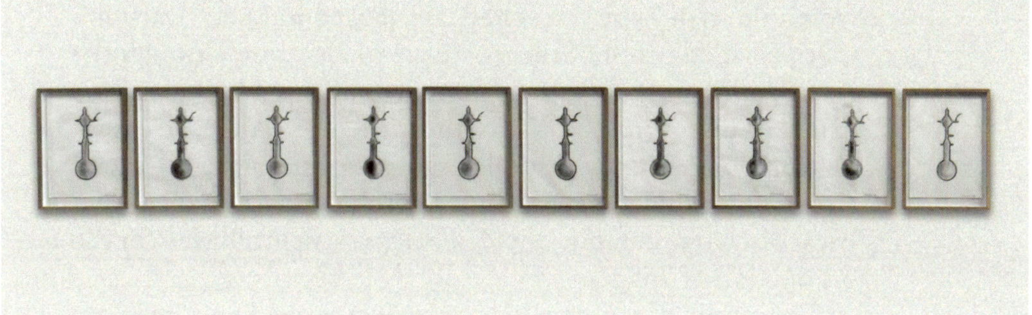

Judgments on Thomson's e/m Tube, 1996
set of 10 drawings, black pencil and stump on grid paper
28 × 21 cm (each piece unframed)
MAMCO collection, gift of Christian Bernard
inv.: 1996–492 (1 to 10)

The British physicist, Joseph John Thomson, invented and perfected the e/m Tube,[66] a spherical tube, containing a vacuum, that provided proof of the existence of electrons through the visualization of their path of motion as affected by a magnetic field. His discovery gave rise to the cathode-ray tube, an essential component in the first television sets, in which a bundle of electrons produces images. The e/m Tube showed that an electrical discharge combined with a magnetic field allowed for the production of images.

By means of ten drawings reproducing the first e/m Tube, Rabinowitch makes a "judgment," i.e. an act of thought that settles a question. He is making a judgment on knowledge and experimentation through direct observation, and he is "foregrounding his interest in experimental method and in the materialization of the equilibrium between the abstract scientific world and the concrete-intuitive world."[67]

Like the spirit level and the plumb bob, Galileo's sector, the Fortin-type barometer, and Henry Cavendish's precision scales, Thomson's e/m Tube "must indeed be included in the list of scientific instruments whose construction can provide a definition for a judgment on rational/empirical procedures."[68]

Exhibition history

L'Éternel Détour – Summer sequence 2011 – Presentation of the collections 2011 (Summer) – June 8, 2011–September 18, 2011

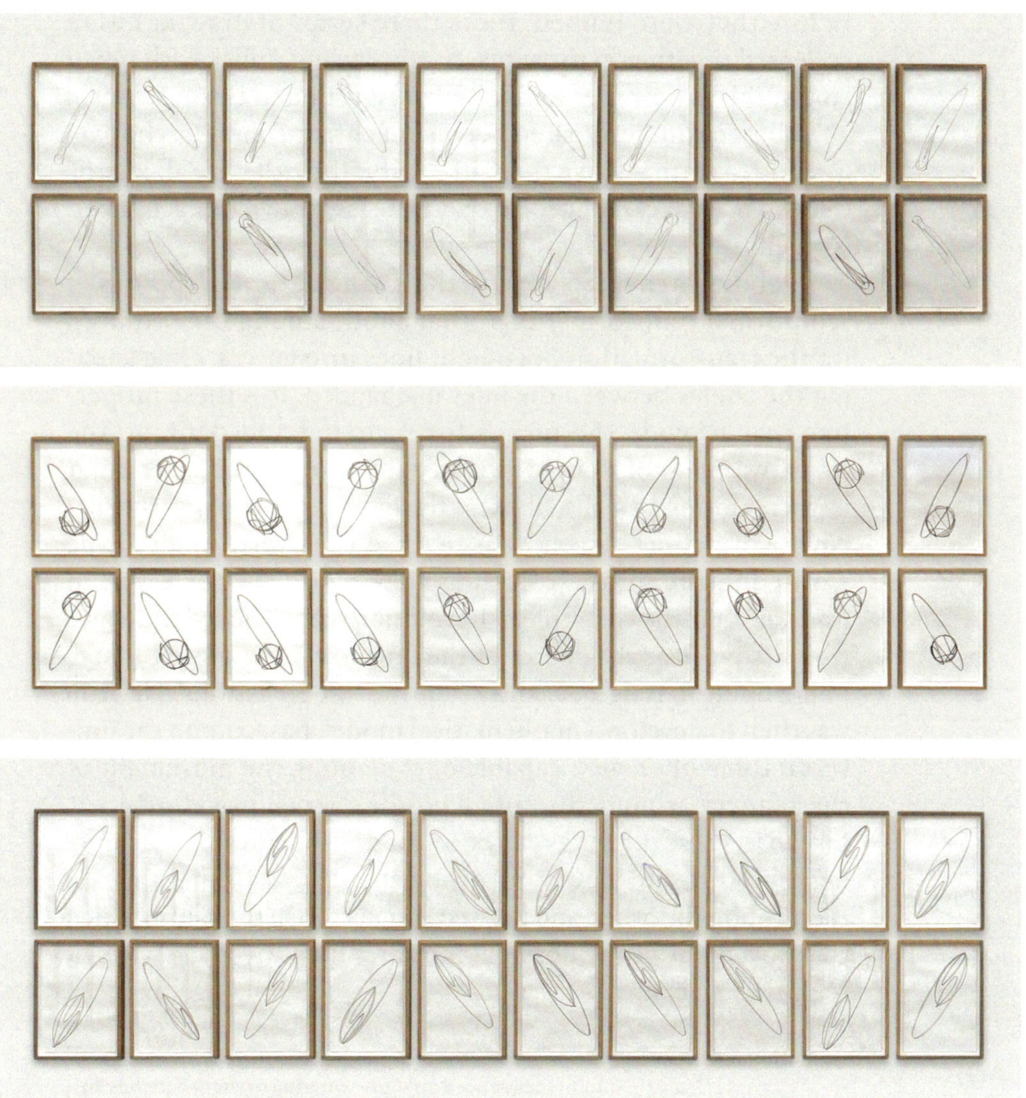

Judgments on Conformal Transformations, February 1996
set of 20 drawings, pastel on paper
29.7 × 21 cm (each piece unframed)
MAMCO collection, gift of Christian Bernard
inv.: 1996–489 (1 to 20)

Judgments on Conformal Transformations, April 1996
set of 20 drawings, pastel on paper
29.7 × 21 cm (each piece unframed)
MAMCO collection, gift of Christian Bernard
inv.: 1996–490 (1 to 20)

Judgments on Conformal Transformations, May 1996
set of 20 drawings, pastel on paper
29.7 × 21 cm (each piece unframed)
MAMCO collection, gift of Christian Bernard
inv.: 1996–491 (1 to 20)

Before they were framed, these three series of drawings were collected together in three plastic display portfolios with typed labels; this is how they had usually been curated by museums.

This ensemble, created between February and March 1996, has both a formal and a thematic unity: the titles are all identical, and in each case the form that appears, drawn on each sheet, is an ellipse.

Rabinowitch refers here to the mathematical properties of "conformal transformations" that allow, among other things, for the transformation of straight lines into curves while keeping the angles between the lines unchanged. It is these properties that provide the means for studying and defining the transformation of a circle into an ellipse. In this connection, it is worth noting that the ellipse is the figure, symbolizing the discovery of heliocentrism, that marked the overturning of the world and the universe such as they had been perceived in Antiquity, i.e. the Copernican Revolution that removed the world from its place at the center of the universe, giving rise to huge philosophical, religious, and scientific repercussions. Newton was then to develop a mathematical model, based upon the universal force of gravity, capable of explaining the movement of the planets around the sun according to elliptical orbits.[69] Likewise, these drawings can be located within the relation uniting sculpture and viewer, involving the attraction that the one exerts upon the other, and located equally too in the way in which the movement of the observer modifies how any given work of sculpture is seen.

Exhibition history

L'Éternel Détour – Summer sequence 2011 – Presentation of the collections 2011 (Summer)– June 8, 2011–September 18, 2011

Notes

1 Robert Morris: "Much of the new sculpture makes a positive value of large size. It is one of the necessary conditions of avoiding intimacy." "Notes on Sculpture. Part 2," *Artforum*, October 1966, p. 21.

2 Cited in Rosalind E. Krauss, *Passages in Modern Sculpture*, (New York: Viking, 1977) p. 3.

3 Ibid., p. 4. For Krauss, these ideas apply generally to modern and contemporary sculpture.

4 Ibid., p. 5.

5 Royden Rabinowitch: "All my constructions are functions of the standard machines any fabrication factory employs in the 'forming' section of their plants, sometimes but rarely assisted by the standard machines any fabrication factory employs in the 'machining' section of their plants. And indeed, my constructions are mostly functions of standard 'hand presses,' namely the 'break press' and the 'rolling press.'" Email to the author, July 12, 2021.

6 David Smith: "Their yard had the locale and nostalgia of my first ironworks of 1934 in Brooklyn, except on a grand scale, and here what hung or was to be found was mine. Plates of varying weights lay rusting in the yard. I used them, but I had to hurry. A salvage crew was in several days a week with their gondolas and switch engine for heavy scrap to feed the melt at Cornegliano. Had I failed to take it first, I could have gone to the mill and got it new..." *David Smith in Italy*, Exh. cat., (Milan: PradaMilanoarte, 1995), p. 34.

7 Jaromir Jedlinski: "I called Rabinowitch's work sculptural investigations because of the duality of the method. Hitherto, the act of analyzing logical rather than visual structure by way of either anthropomorphic or non-anthropomorphic forms has not resulted in personal artistic realizations... Rabinowitch's aspiration is to find a way of communicating with the viewer on the level not of the intellectual but of elemental somatic experiences. In effect, a new object of art created, a metaphor for the possibilities of understanding leading to the basis of building the work of art." "Sculptural Investigations," in *Royden Rabinowitch, Skulpturen 1990*, (Bern: Kunstmuseum Bern/Benteli Verlag Bern, 1990), p. 40.

8 Royden Rabinowitch: "Jonathan Swift, around the time of Newton, coined the term "excremental vision" to attack idealism, perhaps the first stunningly powerful judgment of any vital artist, on the depravity of idealism. And, throughout my life as an artist, I have followed Swift's lead in this matter with all the strength and cunning I possess. ... all my work follows from a foundation I established in Toronto between 1962 and 1965, a foundation of five direct constructions, namely:
1. *Universal Plumb Bob* (Address to David Smith's "Five Units Equal"), 1962
2. *Divided Conic* (Address to Rodtchenko's "Construction of Distance"), 1962
3. *Weighted Conic* (Address to Giacometti's "Nose"), 1962
4. *Barrel Construction* (Address to Tatlin's "Moon on Stage"), 1963
5. *Greased Cone* (Address to Brancusi's "Portrait of J. Joyce"), 1965
These five constructions dramatize five primitive conditions that all direct constructions must satisfy if they really are limited to exposing the irresolvable friction between any direct observer (the local/somatic operator) and any consensual norm (the rational/empirical operator). Around 2000, I was struck with the necessity of establishing a new foundation based on the last work of the old foundation (*Greased Cone*, 1965). The central primitive condition that all direct constructions must satisfy if they really are limited to exposing the irresolvable friction between any local/somatic operator and any rational/empirical operator. Surprisingly and highly gratifying to me, this new foundation, after a twenty year struggle, has recently been established. So your questions come to me at the right time when I can answer them with a degree of clarity. Usually, as you know, a question to an artist is like a red flag to a bull -- the artist, like the bull, ending up dead. Unusually, in our case, I can answer your questions free from the fear of being butchered in the ring of ideas.

When I came of age in 1955 (the year of Einstein's death) I was introduced to the scholarly literature on the Holocaust (mainly Gilbert and Friedlander) by my uncle, a pathologist and refugee from Austria. With my uncle Lenz Mautner's help I gradually started, bit by bit, to understand the very etiology of anti-semitism. And this etiology is, in its most general form, a history of idealism which unsurprisingly accounts for the content of all my work, for the fact that every one of my constructions through two or three axes is a dramatic instance of a struggle against idealism, a dramatic instance of a struggle against the denial of the fact that whatever our future holds for us it will never include a resolution of the friction between any direct observer (any local/somatic operator) and any consensual norm (any rational/empirical operator). Around this time I was also introduced to the scholarly literature on the scientific revolution and its build-up (mainly Burtt and Koyré) and to Panofsky's *Early Nederlandish Painting* by Abraham Robinson, a friend of my parents and a refugee mathematician who patiently, over a number of years, talked me through these books, hugely reinforcing my faith in my ability to engage in the struggle against idealism, to engage in this struggle with the things I found around me, with the things around me that were profoundly interesting to me. In the summer of 1957, my father took me to Manhattan to see David Smith's retrospective at MOMA, and finally I was on the path that I would follow for the rest of my life." Email to the author, July 2, 2021.

9 Royden Rabinowitch, letter to Alain Rérat, August 17, 1995.

10 Between 2010 and 2012, Rabinowitch produced several works with the title *Stan and Ollie* or "The Main Reason Each is Incomplete is the Existence of the Other." Roland Nachtigäller interprets this important reference for the artist: "For many years they have been a recurrent feature of Rabinowitch's works and personify for him the ontological contradiction around which his entire thinking and work revolve. They are the almost perfect embodiment of the ironic polarity of faith and doubt, of values and facts, and for Rabinowitch function as a translation of a highly philosophical analysis into popular culture. In their joint dealings, Stan and Ollie's opposed and confident applications of logic and instinctive action are locked in a constant battle with the dangers of the world and as such they can only manage imperfectly and ironically together and remain inextricably dependent on one another." *Royden Rabinowitch*, Ghent, Exh. cat., (Gent: Mer Paper Kuntshalle, 2014), p. 40.

11 Royden Rabinowitch: "My titles are just aspects of the poetry I assume I'm involved with and my involvement with music is but another aspect of that poetry." Email to the author, July 2, 2021.

12 The exhibitions at the Furka Pass (1983–1996) have become mythical in Switzerland, and this is due in part to the fame of the sixty or so artists who responded, in their turn, to the invitation of the Neuchâtel gallery owner Marc Hostettler, and due in part also to the isolation of the location. Situated far from any urban centers, at an altitude of 2,429 meters, and accessible for only three months in the year, the site guaranteed to works that were often ephemeral the aura of a special occasion. Such was indeed the case at the inaugural performance on June 24, 1983 when James Lee Byars, dressed in a golden suit, with a top hat and patent leather shoes, his face covered by a black scarf, poured onto one of the mountain's boulders a droplet of black perfume, its odour disappearing swiftly in the wind.

13 Royden Rabinowitch, "Collected Notes," in *Royden Rabinowitch, Sculpture 1962/1992*, (The Hague: Gemeentemuseum, 1992), p. 360.

14 Ibid.

15 Ibid., p. 361.

16 Ibid., p. 372.

17 Ibid., p. 371.

18 Max Roach was an outstanding drummer who firmly established the drum solo as part of jazz repertoire.

19 Royden Rabinowitch: "To me, the most fundamental and powerful expression of clear thinking in the realm of the concrete came from the actively working great jazz drummers of the day, also it seemed to me that a conic rose and fell like the sound of a drum." "Collected Notes," in *Royden Rabinowitch, Sculpture 1962/1992*, op. cit., p. 352.

20 David Smith was the first to have conferred rights upon rusted steel. For his *Voltri* series, immense anthropomorphic figures, inspired by Roman ruins, that he created in the summer of 1950, Smith used metal plates, keeping the natural colour of the rust, and breaking with his usual practice of covering the metal with paint. Robert Smithson writes, "As 'technology' and 'industry' began to become an ideology in the New York Art World in the late '50s and early '60s, the private studio notions of 'craft' collapsed. The products of industry and technology began to have an appeal to the artist who wanted to work like a 'steel welder' or a 'laboratory technician.' This valuation of the material products of heavy industry, first developed by David Smith and later by Anthony Caro, led to a fetish for steel and aluminum as a medium (painted or unpainted)." "A Sedimentation of the Mind: Earth Projects," reprinted in *Art in Theory 1900–2000*, ed. Charles Harrison & Paul Wood, (Malden, MA: Blackwell, 2003), p. 878. In Rabinowitch, there is no fetishization in the use of the material.

21 Royden Rabinowitch, cited by Jaromir Jedlinski in *Royden Rabinowitch, Skulpturen 1990*, op. cit., p. 49.

22 Royden Rabinowitch: "The third phase regarding the development of axiomatic mathematics comprises the application of the theory of proportion to geometrical methods of the mean propositional. To judge this I casually joined a rolled half-conic (not truncated) to a developed, truncated half-conic. The lengths of the conics were not equal, the slopes were equal. A radius was shared between them leaving an end radius to be compared with the other end radius zero. This affected no visual comparison or proportion between ends thus established a radius compared with the over-all length of the addition parts – The Greeks carried out the construction of the mean proportional by using some very elementary facts about similarity together with a theory of Thales' pertaining to the angle in a semi-circle (which states that the angle in a semicircle is always a right angle). This construction is titled 'For Max Roach.'" Ibid., p. 50–51.

23 Royden Rabinowitch: "I approached the origins of abstract thinking through two avenues: 1. Through the study of beginnings of the Greek theory of music because the oldest phase in the development of Greek geometry (the first truly abstract thinking) came from the musical theory proportion, i.e. all the technical terms of the later general mathematical theory originated in the musical theory, and 2. Through the epistemological discussion carried out mainly by Einstein and Poincaré at the turn of the century (this discussion perhaps surprisingly, was in no way technical however demanding)." *Royden Rabinowitch—Who Ordered This?*, Exh. cat., (La Gomera: Atelier del Sur, 1990) (interview Royden Rabinowitch/Jan Hoet), n. p.

24 Rabinowitch is interested in bells—uniting sculpture and sound – and notably in the "Tsar Bell", cast between 1733 and 1735. The bell cracked during a fire in 1737, and was left lying in pieces outside the church for which it had been built, never having produced any sound. "...the open, grounded, cracked bell (a bell in name only) became a metaphor for the assumptions applying after the 17th century." "Collected Notes," in *Royden Rabinowitch, Sculpture 1962/1992*, op. cit., p. 346.

25 Royden Rabinowitch: "To get hints from the modern history of body-making in sculpture, I concentrated on a certain analysis of Rodin, mainly that the appearances in Rodin were so new because they were more about parts (discreteness) than previous carvings or modelings in the development (with more and more discrete treatments) from Rodin to Brancusi to Giacometti to David Smith. Further clues were provided by the transition from Picasso to Tatlin (from parts arranged symbolically to simply parts arranged around axes) and from the two sculptures of Boccioni: "Unique Forms of Continuity in Space" and "Development of a Bottle in Space." *Royden Rabinowitch—Who Ordered This?*, op. cit., n. p.

26 Royden Rabinowitch, "Collected Notes," in *Royden Rabinowitch, Sculpture 1962/1992*, op. cit., p. 355.

27 Ibid., p. 323.

28 David Smith does this in his series *Tanktotem* (1950). As Rosalind Krauss describes it: "The lower disk, fashioned from a tank top or boiler head, serves as the bottom part of the figure's torso, while the upper disk caps the sculpture with a flange-like representation of the totemic head." *Passages,* op. cit., p. 147.

29 Royden Rabinowitch, "Collected Notes," in *Royden Rabinowitch, Sculpture 1962/1992,* op. cit., p. 358.

30 Ibid. p. 358–359.

31 Royden Rabinowitch, Email to the author, June 23, 2021.

32 Rabinowitch makes clear that, up to Smith, sculptors had been preoccupied with the development of the anthropomorphic form, i.e. constructions dealing with the representation of the human form. His own work, however, had moved to a more advanced stage, involving "time itself." He describes his barrel constructions as, "...collected moments... (they) constitute the internal sense of duration." His work alludes to the human body, yet it avoids Smith's anthropomorphic imagery. Ibid., p. 359.

33 Jan Hoet, "Royden Rabinowitch's 'Handed Manifolds' Revisited," in *Royden Rabinowitch, Skulpturen 1990,* op. cit., p. 13.

34 Robert Morris: "Properties which are not read as detail in large works become detail in small works." art. cit., p. 21.

35 Philippe Sollers, "In May 1928, Brancusi produced at first six sketches (of Joyce) in a realist style (three profiles and three frontal images), capturing his visitor's physiognomy through the customary rapid notations. He had, therefore, right from the beginning, the circular motif from the round glasses. Confronted with the disappointment of his patrons in this commission who were looking for a more abstract design, Brancusi drew a symbolic spiral. This was to be accepted, and the piece would later be titled, in 1954, *Symbol Of Joyce." Portrait de Joyce par Brancusi,* Pileface.com article 2402, consulted April 22, 2021.

36 The exhibition *Equilibrium? Royden Rabinowitch – Historical Turning Points and Artist's Solidarity* took place in January 2014 at the Golden Thread Gallery in Belfast. The show included a publication by Royden Rabinowitch that included Beuys' last multiple, *Joyce with Sled* (1985), along with *Greased Cone* as an address to Brancusi's *Portrait of James Joyce* ca. 1928.

37 Harald Szeemann, Exhibition flyer for *GAS,* (Bordeaux: CAPC, 1993).

38 We are grateful to Frank Maes, artistic director of the Emergent exhibition space, for all of the information pertaining to this performance.

39 Royden Rabinowitch, "Collected Notes," in *Royden Rabinowitch, Sculpture 1962/1992,* op. cit., p. 363.

40 In this 1965 text, Donald Judd examines the three-dimensionality that emerged out of painting: "Half or more of the best new work in the last few years has been neither painting nor sculpture. Usually it has been related, closely or distantly, to one or the other. The work is diverse, and much in it that is not in painting and sculpture is also diverse... Three dimensions are real space. That gets rid of the problem of illusionism and of literal space, space in and around marks and colors—which is riddance of one of the salient and most objectionable relics of European art." "Specific Objects," reprinted in *Art in Theory 1900–1990,* op. cit., p. 824.

41 Hot bluing is a metallurgical process that produces a mainly blue-black finish to the steel plate, with occasionally a red ochre tinge.

42 *Royden Rabinowitch, Skulpturen 1990,* op. cit., p. 13.

43 Rosalind Krauss, *Passages,* op. cit., p. 157.

44 David Smith, "The use of arc welding to develop aesthetics is strictly twentieth century... It is the most desirable method of joining metal—here in sculpture—just as it was when I welded M7 tank destroyers and locomotives at the American Locomotive Works... The arc welding fabrication of sculpture has caused certain changes in aesthetic concepts just as it has in industrial design. The aim is no longer to imitate a casting. The art concept must be in unity with the method—a recognition of the change of forces, knowledge of the material and respect for the virtues of the method and a creative vision towards the yet unlimited possibilities which the new method has opened... I first used arc welding as a conceptual means in sculpture in 1937." David Smith: *Collected Writings, Lectures, and Interviews,* ed. Susan J. Cooke, (Oakland, California: University of California Press, 2018), pp. 71–72.

45 Royden Rabinowitch, "I do give technical drawings to the fabricator or sometimes just a set of calculations to the fabricator and also participate in the fabrication of my work. All the surfaces developed or rolled you see in my work are approximations of some calculation (prediction) and sometimes the prediction is falsified by my intuitive expectations which makes the whole process wild and exciting to me. This is just to say that I start by assuming I have some grasp of what I am doing and end up surprised that I have no grasp of what I am doing. If this surprise is absent this is the sign to me that I have failed, that I have to start over to attempt to surprise myself. This surprise is the whole ball of wax, the real victory over vestiges of idealism that always are there within me. This surprise is at the very center of my struggle against idealism." Email to the author, July 4, 2021.

46 Royden Rabinowitch, "Collected Notes," in *Royden Rabinowitch, Sculpture 1962/1992,* op. cit., p. 369.

47 Ibid., p. 368.

48 Carl Andre, for whom the ideal sculpture would be a road, conceived the latter in solely horizontal terms.

49 Jan Hoet, "A sand blasted steel plate in the form of an irregular, convex polygon is divided into triangular sectors by rays connecting the vertices with a point on one of the sides. Along these rays the plate is folded into something like a shell-shape, so that all sides of the polygon, except the one containing the point of intersection, are touching the ground. The folding operation actually transforms the plate into a very low, oblique, irregular and incomplete sided and faceted conic with the intersection of rays as its highest point (never higher than 10 cm!). Besides the "Handed Manifold" is always complemented with one or more so-called "added limits." They consist of trapezoidal plates, congruent with the lower part of the triangular facet they partially cover, thus duplicating it locally and doubling the plate's gauge, i.e. thickness." "Royden Rabinowitch's 'Handed Manifolds' Revisited," in *Royden Rabinowitch, Skulpturen 1990,* op. cit., p. 18.

50 Thomas McEvilley, 'Spuren, Skulpturen und Monumente ihrer präzisen Reise,' *Artforum,* April 1986, pp. 120–121.

51 Jan Hoet: "This captivating confusion and irresolvable equivocality is as essential to the aesthetic radiation of these works as the convergence of beauty and enigma in Moebius' band. It is almost inevitable to consider the reduced three-dimensionality and the almost totalitarian regime of the formative principle of gravity as a manifestation of the bend with spread horizontalism, a hunger for the 'floorness', that was once duly described as a "concerted assault on the axiomatic verticality in sculpture', and which can arguably be considered the

counterpart of the obsession with 'flatness' in (American) Painting after the second World War." "Royden Rabinowitch's 'Handed Manifolds' Revisited," in *Royden Rabinowitch, Skulpturen 1990*, op. cit., p. 18. See also Robert Pincus-Witten, *Postminimalism,* (New York: Norristown/Milano, 1977) p. 23.

52 *Rotation and Translation of the Top* (1983) is the first example of this order. It was created for the Sarabhai family in Ahmedabad, India. Rabinowitch concentrated here on the top/bottom property, producing a series of sculptures with "a double curvature… the fundamental operations of translation and rotation being applied to the top." Royden Rabinowitch, "Collected Notes," in *Royden Rabinowitch, Sculpture 1962/1992*, op. cit., p. 386.

53 Emanuel Feuermann's technique was so innovative that a dissertation has been written on it. See Brinton Smith, *The Physical and Interpretative Technique of Emanuel Feuermann*, https://www.cellobello.org/cello-blog/artistic-vision/emanuel-feuermann-and-the-art-of-phrasing-by-brinton-averil-smith/, consulted 21 July, 2021. In his dissertation, Brinton Smith writes: "Feuermann's right arm is held in a fairly simple manner. Neither the elbow or wrist is raised, so there is the impression of a straight, smooth descending line. It may be that his shoulder is slightly raised, facilitating the relatively natural position of the wrist and elbow, but it is impossible to be sure from the film. Feuermann's arm is bent at the elbow, as is typical for cellists, but Feuermann maintains this bend throughout the bow, almost never allowing the arm to fully straighten. His wrist raises up and down during the course of up and down-bows, respectively. While the wrist rises gradually throughout the course of the up-bow, it often lowers immediately with the start of the down-bow. This raising and lowering of the wrist is active and noticeable, but never looks unnatural or extreme."

54 Royden Rabinowitch: "…within a half rotation I wanted the full possibilities of the full rotation, making clear that against a wall as well as a floor, space is somatic and local not abstract and extended. Any analysis regarding this problem proved hopeless and finally the thing was resolved by dwelling on the operations of any cellist, i.e. the discrete fingering above and behind the continuous bowing, involved in the articulating of sounds." Ibid., p.393.

55 Rudi Fuchs, "Bending the Mind," in *Royden Rabinowitch, Skulpturen 1990*, op. cit., p. 11.

56 Royden Rabinowitch: "After I made the 'Handed Manifold,' the first somatic construction, I wondered for about two years if there was a faster, easier way to make a somatic construction, i.e. could I make a somatic drawing? I certainly have never had any interest in developing parallels between the appearances of drawing and sculpture. I wondered what a somatic drawing would look like if it could be made and started to concentrate on the back/front or closed/open property of the 'Handed Manifold.' This property was the stumbling block because there is no back/front to a vertical plane – although all the other somatic descriptions can easily be accommodated by arrangements of lines on a vertical plane. I thought finally that the back/front property is easily conceived of as closed/open, and the closed/open description is easily conceived of as discontinuous for the observers, i.e. closed, and continuous for observers, i.e. open, and discontinuous and continuous lines are easily drawn so I thought I had a way to make a somatic drawing." *Royden Rabinowitch—Who Ordered This?*, op. cit., n. p.

57 Through a similar poetic impetus, Joyce conceived the opening of *Ulysses* after spending six nights in one of the Dublin Martello Towers, a site that is now a museum dedicated to the writer.

58 Royden Rabinowitch, Email to the author, July 2, 2021.

59 Royden Rabinowitch: "I was dwelling on the things I have just talked about and mulling over the quality of stillness I'd sensed from the tombs of the Dukes of Burgundy. This quality came only if you didn't move and so I sat for many hours day after day, and just moved my eyes around and up and down, sometimes stopping to look and then moving them again, and I started to realize that this motion was the same as the motion involved when I quickly closed a plane curve, i.e. when I quickly drew a closed curve on a plane. I was still confused about my sense of deep space when I didn't move—this seemed like the full space of ordinary experience. Then I realized that seeing in depth when not moving is only a memory of when the body was moving. When the body starts moving, the vertical plane of experience vanishes and the full space of ordinary experience takes over. Then I knew the vertical plane of experience (as distinct from 2–space as the full space of ordinary experience was distinct from 3–space) must be a casual, buoyant (eyes float) map or guide that static observers can follow with their eyes. This map could have nothing to do with weight or force or material (as these are associated only with the limited operations of a moving body creating the ordinary full space of experience). This casual guide would include four qualities: floating, devices, like eyes translated from bottom to middle to top; rotations of the eyes, around and from side to side and up and down; concentrations or stops; and the most passive, casual execution possible (approximating the true nature of stillness). All motions of eyes would be connected together and yet never cease to operate separately. Because I became aware of the stop motion, the drawing of the casual, buoyant map would precede the drawing of the concentration or stoppages of the casual, buoyant map. After I spent more time just sitting around in Cambridge, I became pretty aware of the main locations the floating devices should occupy and then I brought in all my experience of making things." *Royden Rabinowitch—Who Ordered This ?*, op. cit., np.

60 Ibid.

61 Royden Rabinowitch, Email to the author, July 9, 2021.

62 Royden Rabinowitch, Email to the author, July 9, 2021.

63 Royden Rabinowitch, Email to the author, July 9, 2021.

64 Roman Kurzmeyer, *Royden Rabinowitch*, Ghent, Exh. cat., (Gent: Mer Paper Kuntshalle, 2014), p. 19.

65 Royden Rabinowitch: "The coloured and graphite treatments of planes… I can't remember how many things of this kind I've actually done and as for the size of these things they are more or less the extent of my reach, which is all I am concerned with. I think colour matters because it's the one thing that can't be incorporated into any possible physical theory, which is perfectly explained by Heisenberg's dismantling of Goethe's colour theory." Email to the author, July 2, 2021.

66 e/m is the ratio of the charge of an electron to the mass of an electron.

67 Hans Theys, *Royden Rabinowitch, Points d'ancrage dans un monde désenchanté*, conversation avec Frank Maes à propos de Royden Rabinowitch, (Montagne de Miel, 18 janvier 2016). http://hanstheys.ensembles.org/items/royden-rabinowitch-2016-points-d-ancrage-dans-un-monde-desenchante-fr-interview, consulted July 20, 2021.

68 Royden Rabinowitch, Email to the author, July 9, 2021.

69 Royden Rabinowitch: "The *Conformal Transformations* are judgments on a certain mapping scheme only involved with corners in the most general (abstract) sense. A drawing only makes sense to me when I stand still and only my eyes

move...after the space of points was sufficiently established by Descartes to allow Newton to complete the Copernican Revolution, to allow Newton to unify the terrestrial mechanics of Galileo and the celestial mechanics of Kepler, with his invention of his calculus and his invention of his rational/empirical paradigm, which paradigm has not needed altering even up to the present day. It took almost a hundred years for a very great mathematician, Monge, to invent the plan and elevation." Email to the author, July 2, 2021.

|1|0|2|

ROYDEN RABINOWITCH AT MAMCO

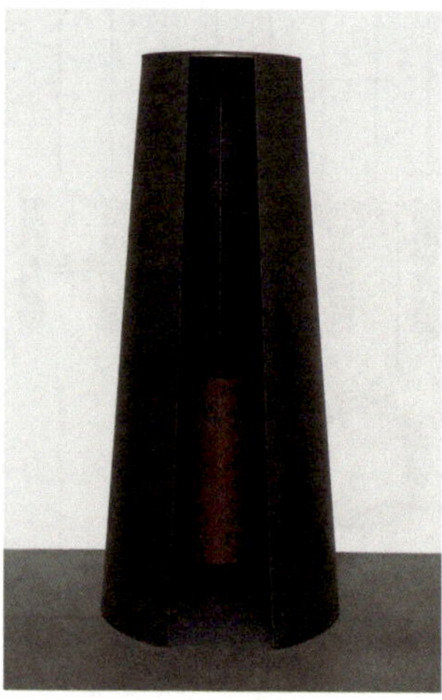

Royden Rabinowitch (*1943)
Initial Address to "Le Nez" (C): Central Order of Things and Events, 1962
1st Judgment on the Basis of Abstract Thinking
Series: FIVE ADDRESSES TO GIACOMETTI'S "LE NEZ" (FIVE JUDGMENTS ON THE BASIS OF ABSTRACT THINKING)
three-piece sculpture, oiled steel
cone: 178.5 (height) × 80 cm (diameter) / rod: 91 cm (length) × 1 cm (diameter) / weight: 59 cm (length) x 25.5 cm (diameter)
MAMCO collection
gift of Max Wandeler
inv.: 2016–420 (1 to 3)

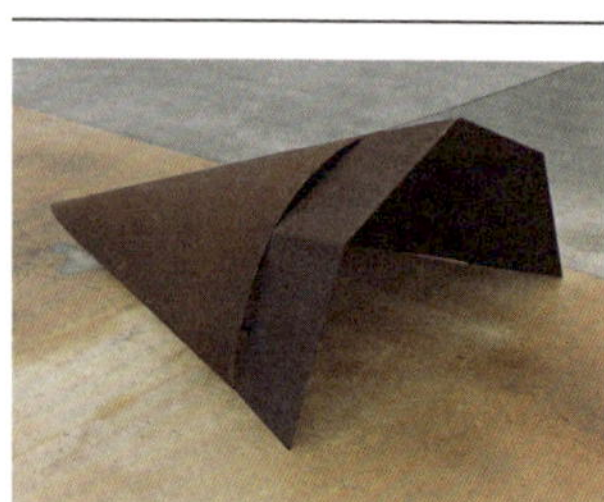

Royden Rabinowitch (*1943)
3rd Homage to Jazz Drummers: For Max Roach, 1962
3rd Judgment on Origins of Abstract Thinking
Series: HOMAGES TO JAZZ DRUMMERS (JUDGMENTS ON ORIGINS OF ABSTRACT THINKING)
two-piece sculpture, rusted steel
73.5 × 225 × 144.5 cm (entire work)
MAMCO collection
gift of Max Wandeler
inv.: 2016–417 (1 to 2)

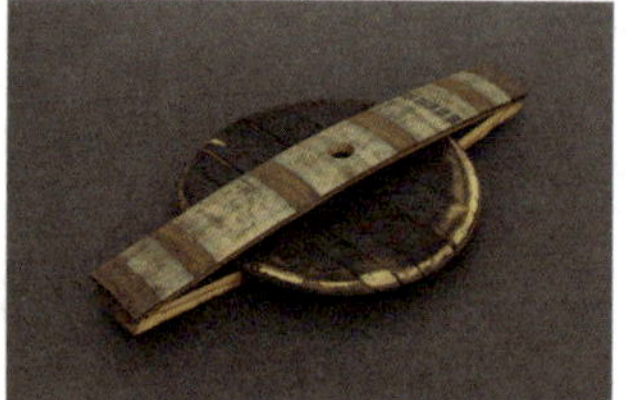

Royden Rabinowitch (*1943)
Barrel Construction (Double Curvature at Right Angles), 1963
Series: BARREL CONSTRUCTIONS— DOUBLE CURVATURES AT RIGHT ANGLES (CONSTRUCTION OF AN INTERNALLY DETERMINED NON-ANTHROPOMORPHIC NON-ARTICULATED BODY)
three-piece sculpture, oak barrel staves and head
10 × 89 × 53 cm (entire work)
MAMCO collection
gift of Max Wandeler
inv.: 2016–413 (1 to 3)

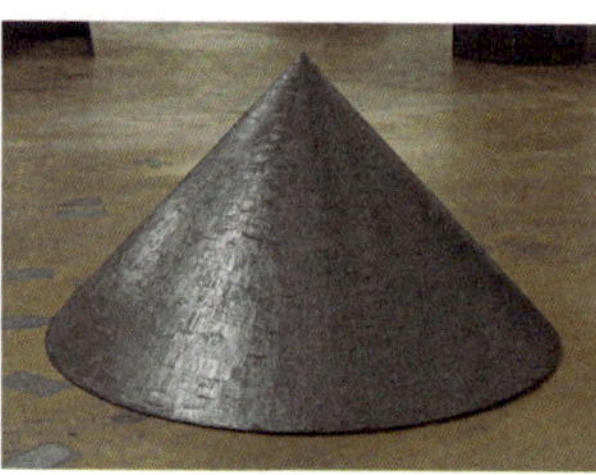

Royden Rabinowitch (*1943)
Discrete Green Vertically Greased Cone, 1965
Series: GREASED CONES (1ST CONSTRUCTION REGARDING INTERNAL CONDITIONS)
steel, grease
120 cm (height) x 168 cm (diameter)
MAMCO collection
gift of Max Wandeler
inv.: 2016–419

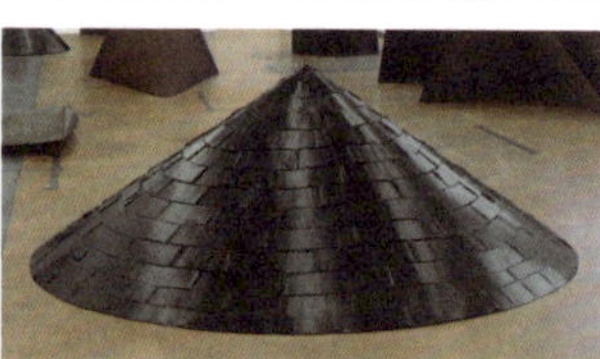

Royden Rabinowitch (*1943)
Dark Grey Horizontally Greased Cone, 1965
Series: GREASED CONES (1ST CONSTRUCTION REGARDING INTERNAL CONDITIONS)
steel, grease
105 (height) x 274 cm (diameter)
MAMCO collection
gift of Max Wandeler
inv.: 2016–429

Royden Rabinowitch (*1943)
Hollow Panel, 1966
Series: HOLLOW PANELS (2ND CONSTRUCTION REGARDING INTERNAL CONDITIONS)
blued steel
31 × 30.5 cm
MAMCO collection
gift of Max Wandeler
inv.: 2016–436

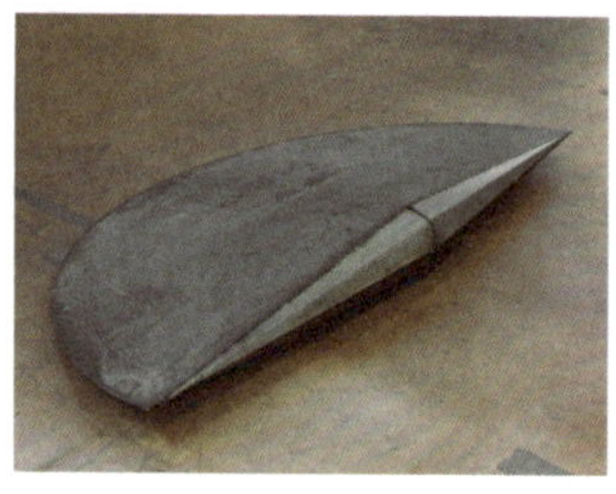

Royden Rabinowitch (*1943)
Conic Turnover, 1967
Series: CONIC TURNOVERS (3RD CONSTRUCTION REGARDING INTERNAL CONDITIONS)
Cold-rolled steel
22 × 204.5 × 106.5 cm
MAMCO collection
gift of Max Wandeler
inv.: 2016–416

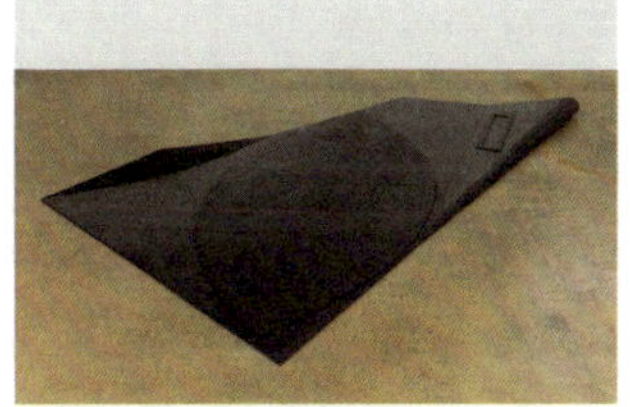

Royden Rabinowitch (*1943)
Karakorum (IV), 1968–1971
Series: *KARAKORUM—SYNTHETIC CONSTRUCTION (SYNTHESIS OF PREVIOUS WORK)*
oiled steel
7 × 162 × 290 cm
MAMCO collection
gift of Max Wandeler
inv.: 2016–422

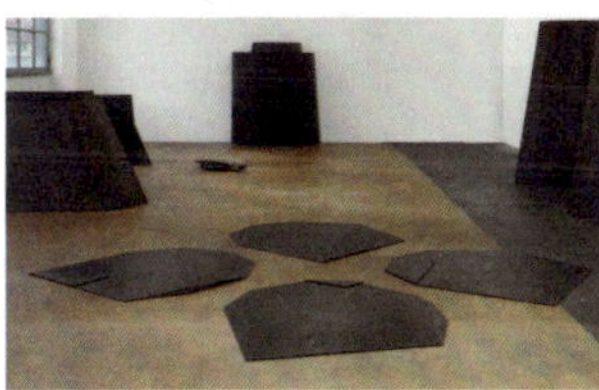

Royden Rabinowitch (*1943)
7 Manifolds in 4 Locations with Varied Handed Additions, 1986
Series: *2ND INTERNALLY DETERMINED FULLY ARTICULATED BODY (HANDED MANIFOLD GROUPS—GENERAL CASES OF HANDED DEVELOPED SURFACES OF ONE SIZE APPLIED TO PLANS) MAINTAINING LOCAL SOMATIC DESCRIPTIONS*
four-piece sculpture, blackened and oiled steel
2 × [2.5 × 132.5 × 116 cm] /
2.5 × 130.5 × 115.5 cm /
2.5 × 130.7 × 118.5 cm
MAMCO collection
gift of Max Wandeler
inv.: 2016–423 (1 to 4)

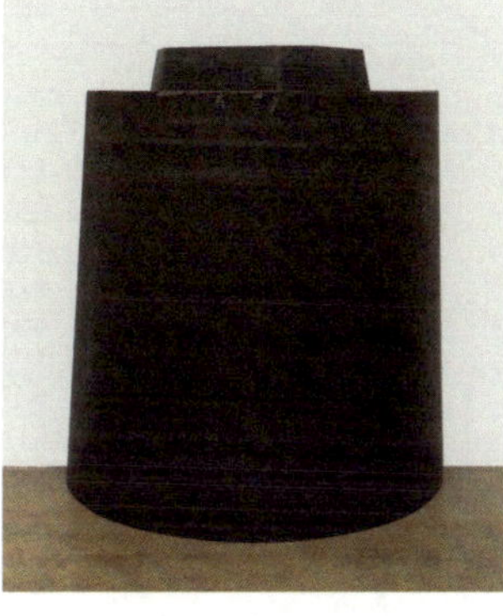

Royden Rabinowitch (*1943)
5th Lesson of Emanuel Feuermann (A), 1987
Series: *3RD INTERNALLY DETERMINED FULLY ARTICULATED BODY (LESSONS OF EMANUEL FEUERMANN—SPECIAL CASES OF HANDED DEVELOPED SURFACES OF TWO SIZES APPLIED TO AN ELEVATION MAINTAINING LOCAL SOMATIC DESCRIPTIONS)*
two-piece sculpture, oiled steel
166.50 × 143 × 76 cm (entire work)
MAMCO collection
gift of Max Wandeler
inv.: 2016–414 (1 to 2)

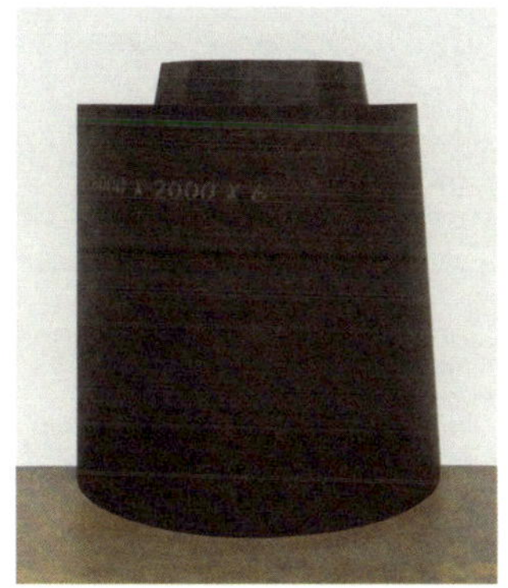

Royden Rabinowitch (*1943)
5th Lesson of Emanuel Feuermann (B), 1987
Series: *3RD INTERNALLY DETERMINED FULLY ARTICULATED BODY (LESSONS OF EMANUEL FEUERMANN—SPECIAL CASES OF HANDED DEVELOPED SURFACES OF TWO SIZES APPLIED TO AN ELEVATION MAINTAINING LOCAL SOMATIC DESCRIPTIONS)*
two-piece sculpture, oiled steel
168.5 × 153.5 × 77 cm (entire work)
MAMCO collection
gift of Max Wandeler
inv.: 2016–428 (1 to 2)

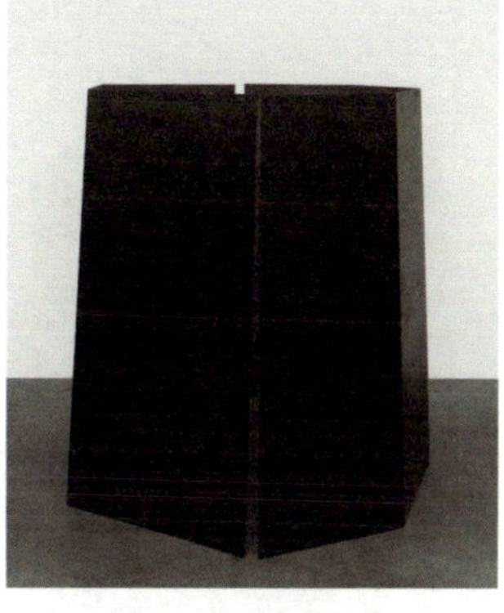

Royden Rabinowitch (*1943)
2nd of Two Opposed Developed Handed Surfaces Applied to Plans and Elevations Maintaining Local Somatic Descriptions, 1987–1988
Series: *TWO OPPOSED DEVELOPED HANDED SURFACES (STARTED 1987) GENERAL CASE OF HANDED DEVELOPED SURFACES APPLIED TO PLANS AND ELEVATIONS MAINTAINING LOCAL SOMATIC DESCRIPTIONS*
two-piece sculpture, rusted and oiled steel
150 × 150 × 151 cm (entire work)
MAMCO collection
gift of Max Wandeler
inv.: 2016–425 (1 to 2)

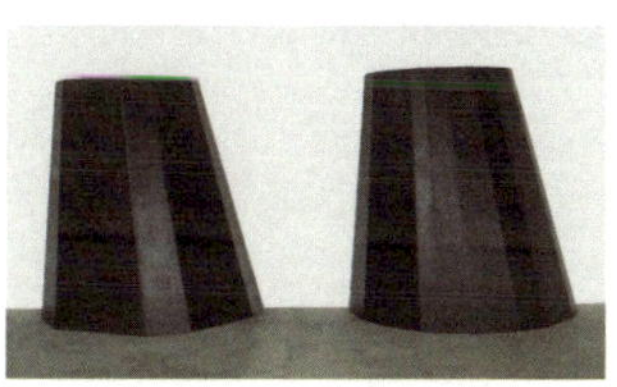

Royden Rabinowitch (*1943)
Disposition of an Internally Determined Fully Articulated Body (1st General Case of Handed Developed Surfaces of One Size Applied to Plans and Elevations Maintaining Local Somatic Descriptions), 1988
Series: *DISPOSITION OF AN INTERNALLY DETERMINED FULLY ARTICULATED BODY (SINGULAR, SPECIAL, AND GENERAL CASES OF HANDED DEVELOPED SURFACES OF ONE SIZE APPLIED TO PLANS AND ELEVATIONS MAINTAINING LOCAL SOMATIC DESCRIPTIONS)*
two-piece sculpture, oiled steel
184.5 × 180 × 102 cm /
184.5 × 182.5 × 102 cm
MAMCO collection
gift of Max Wandeler
inv.: 2016–424 (1 to 2)

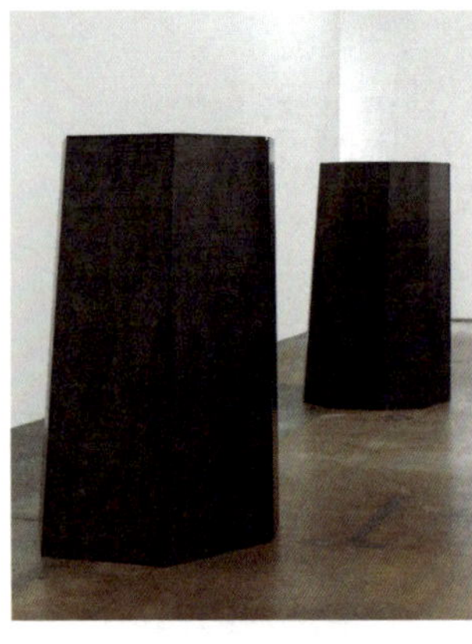

Royden Rabinowitch (*1943)
1st of Six Opposed Handed Developed Same-Sized Surfaces, 1989
(General Case of Opposed Handed Developed Same-Sized Surfaces Applied to Plans and Elevations Maintaining Local Somatic Descriptions—Axes Perpendicular to Wall)
Series: SINGULAR, SPECIAL AND GENERAL CASES OF OPPOSED HANDED DEVELOPED SAME-SIZED SURFACES APPLIED TO PLANS AND ELEVATIONS MAINTAINING LOCAL AND SOMATIC DESCRIPTIONS ORGANIZED REGARDING DIAMETERS AND/OR AXES (STARTED 1987)
six-piece sculpture, blued and oiled steel
182.5 × 122 × 113 cm (each piece)
MAMCO collection
gift of Max Wandeler
inv.: 2016–415 (1 to 6)

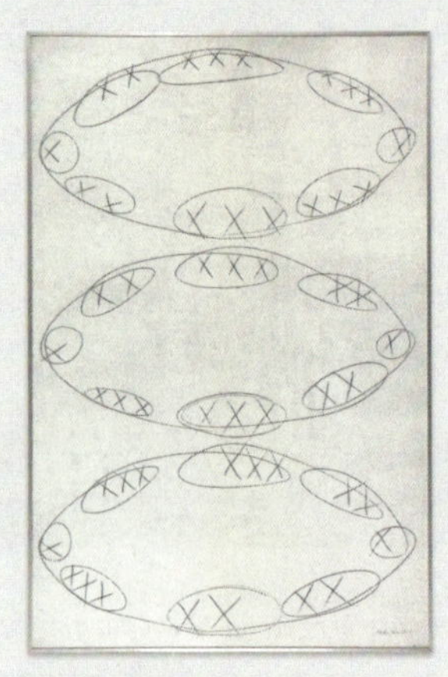

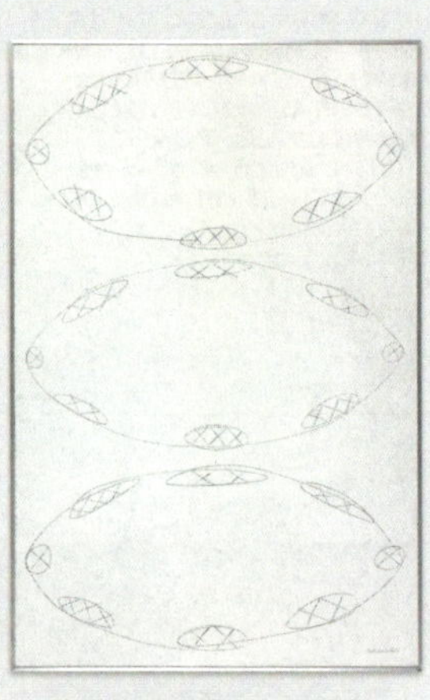

Royden Rabinowitch (*1943)
Singular Case of Handed Operator Bundles Through Two Axes Limited to Local Ocular Descriptions ("Who Ordered This?"), 1990
Series: GUIDES TO THE VERTICAL PLAN OF ORDINARY EXPERIENCE (SINGULAR AND COLOURED CASES OF HANDED OPERATOR BUNDLES THROUGH TWO AXES LIMITED TO LOCAL OCULAR DESCRIPTIONS)
graphite on prepared canvas
300 × 200 cm (framed)
MAMCO collection, gift of Max Wandeler
inv.: 2016–410 / 2016–411

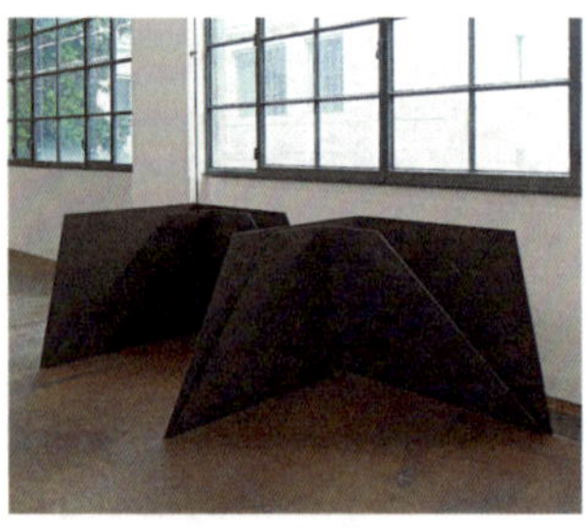

Royden Rabinowitch (*1943)
Double Clutching—After Cecil Taylor, 1991
(Singular Case of Handed Developed Surfaces of Two Sizes Applied to a Plan and Elevation Maintaining Local Somatic Descriptions)
Series: DISPOSITIONS OF AN INTERNALLY DETERMINED FULLY ARTICULATED BODY (SINGULAR, SPECIAL AND GENERAL CASES OF HANDED SURFACES OF TWO SIZES APPLIED TO PLANS AND/OR ELEVATIONS MAINTAINING LOCAL SOMATIC DESCRIPTIONS)
four-piece sculpture, rusted and oiled steel
105 × 142 × 141 cm / 101.5 × 141 × 143 cm (uppermost pieces)
101 × 139 × 139 cm / 101 × 139 × 139 cm (lowermost pieces)
MAMCO collection
gift of Max Wandeler
inv.: 2016–418 (1 to 4)

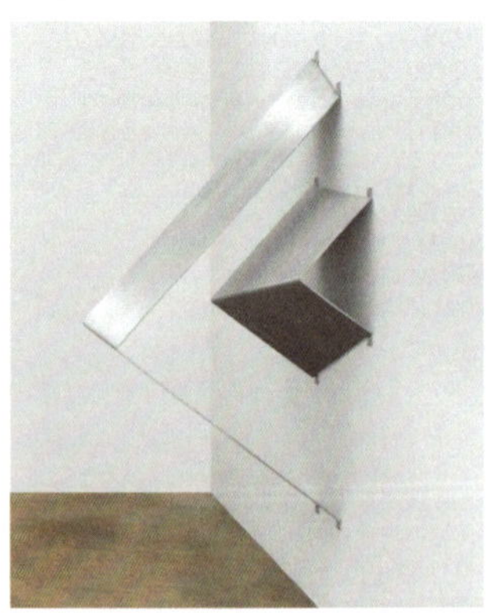

Royden Rabinowitch (*1943)
Open Ice—For Gretzky, 1991
(SINGULAR CASES OF HANDED DEVELOPED SURFACES OF TWO SIZES APPLIED TO THE LIMIT OF THE ELEVATION MAINTAINING LOCAL SOMATIC DESCRIPTIONS)
two-piece sculpture, aluminum
214 × 92 × 107 cm (entire work)
MAMCO collection
gift of Max Wandeler
inv.: 2016–412 (1 to 2)

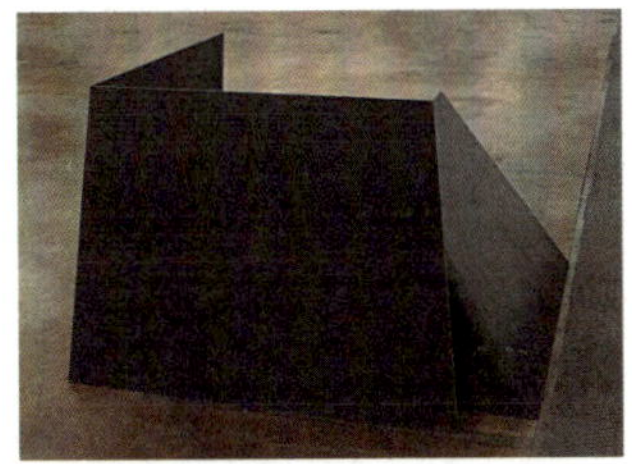

Royden Rabinowitch (*1943)
Double Clutching (for John Coltrane), 1991
Special Case of Handed Developed Surfaces of 2 Sizes Applied to a Plan and Elevation Maintaining Local Somatic Descriptions
Series: DISPOSITION OF AN INTERNALLY DETERMINED FULLY ARTICULATED BODY (SINGULAR, SPECIAL AND GENERAL CASES OF HANDED DEVELOPED SURFACES OF TWO SIZES APPLIED TO PLANS AND/OR ELEVATIONS MAINTAINING LOCAL SOMATIC DESCRIPTIONS)
two-piece sculpture, oiled steel
92 × 126 × 126 cm (uppermost piece) /
76 × 125 × 125 cm (lowermost piece)
MAMCO collection
gift of Max Wandeler
inv.: 2016–427 (1 to 2)

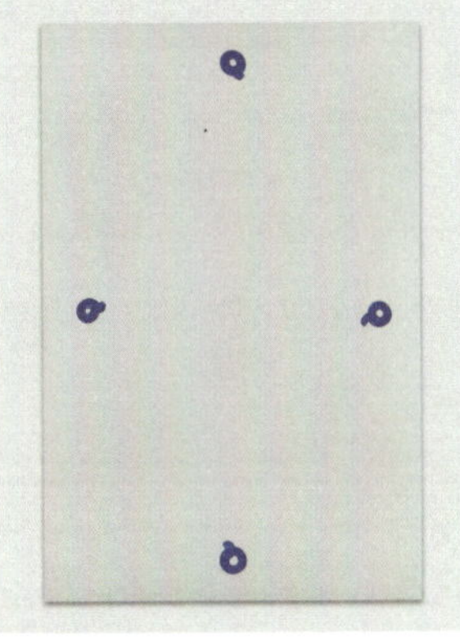

Royden Rabinowitch (*1943)
Coloured Case of Handed Operator Bundles Through Two Axes Limited to Local Ocular Descriptions, 1993
Series: GUIDES TO THE VERTICAL PLAN OF ORDINARY EXPERIENCE—COLOURED CASES OF HANDED OPERATOR BUNDLES THROUGH TWO AXES LIMITED TO LOCAL OCULAR DESCRIPTIONS
acrylic on linen canvas
300 × 200 cm
MAMCO collection
gift of Max Wandeler
inv.: 2016–409

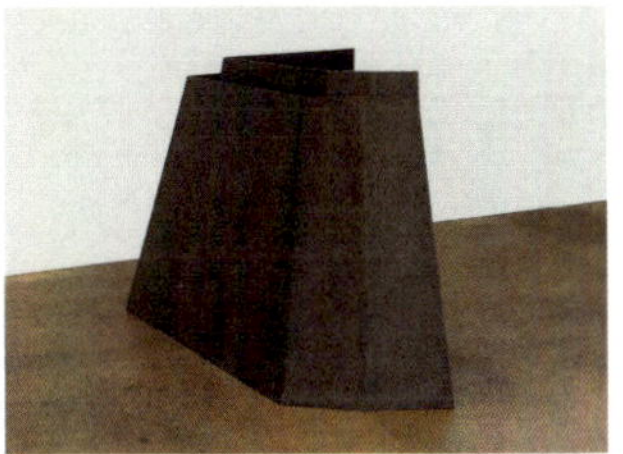

Royden Rabinowitch (*1943)
1st Special Case B of Handed Operator Bundles Through Three Axes Limited to Local Somatic Descriptions (Length Perpendicular to Wall), 1993
Series: GUIDES TO THE FULL SPACE OF ORDINARY EXPERIENCE (SPECIAL AND GENERAL CASES OF HANDED OPERATOR BUNDLES THROUGH THREE AXES LIMITED TO LOCAL SOMATIC DESCRIPTIONS)
two-piece sculpture, steel
107 × 156.50 × 106 cm (uppermost piece) / 98.50 × 204 × 122 cm (lowermost piece)
MAMCO collection
gift of Max Wandeler
inv.: 2016–426 (1 to 2)

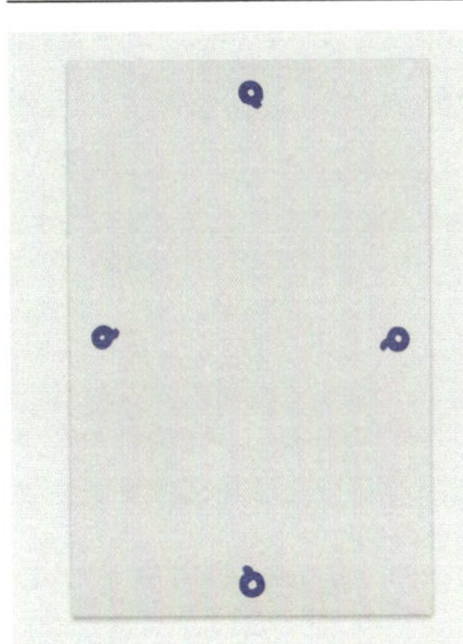

Royden Rabinowitch (*1943)
Coloured Case of Handed Operator Bundles Through Two Axes Limited to Local Ocular Descriptions, 1993
Series: GUIDES TO THE VERTICAL PLAN OF ORDINARY EXPERIENCE—COLOURED CASES OF HANDED OPERATOR BUNDLES THROUGH TWO AXES LIMITED TO LOCAL OCULAR DESCRIPTIONS
acrylic on linen canvas
300 × 200 cm
MAMCO collection
gift of Max Wandeler
inv.: 2016–408

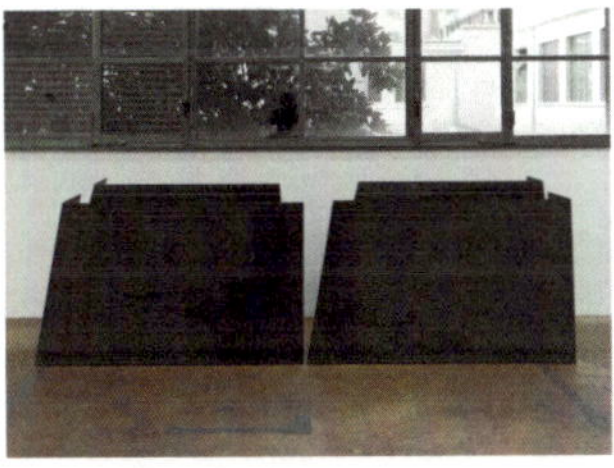

Royden Rabinowitch (*1943)
1st Special Case C of Handed Operator Bundles Through Three Axes Limited to Local Somatic Descriptions (Length Parallel to Wall), 1993
Series: GUIDES TO THE FULL SPACE OF ORDINARY EXPERIENCE (SPECIAL AND GENERAL CASES OF HANDED OPERATOR BUNDLES THROUGH THREE AXES LIMITED TO LOCAL SOMATIC DESCRIPTIONS PARALLEL TO WALL)
four-piece sculpture, oiled steel
101.5 × 137.5 × 35.5 cm (uppermost pieces) /
91 × 148 × 39 cm (lowermost pieces)
MAMCO collection
gift of Max Wandeler
inv.: 2016–421 (1 to 4)

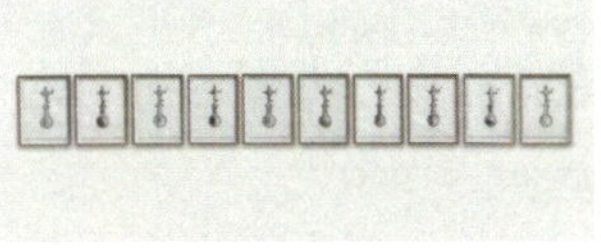

Royden Rabinowitch (*1943)
Judgments on Thomson's e/m Tube, 1996
set of 10 drawings, black pencil and stump on grid paper
28 × 21 cm (each piece unframed)
MAMCO collection
gift of Christian Bernard
inv.: 1996–492 (1 to 10)

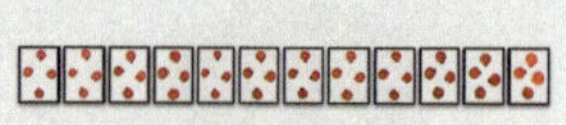

Royden Rabinowitch (*1943)
Judgment on Freedom and Necessity, 1996
set of 12 watercolors on drawing paper
42 × 29.2 cm
(each piece unframed)
MAMCO collection
gift of Christian Bernard
inv.: 1996–493 (1 to 12)

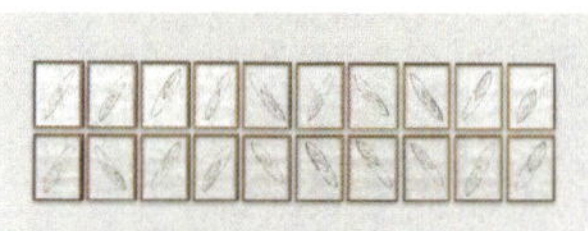

Royden Rabinowitch (*1943)
Judgments on Conformal Transformations, February 1996
set of 20 drawings, pastel on paper
29.7 × 21 cm
(each piece unframed)
MAMCO collection
gift of Christian Bernard
inv.: 1996–489 (1 to 20)

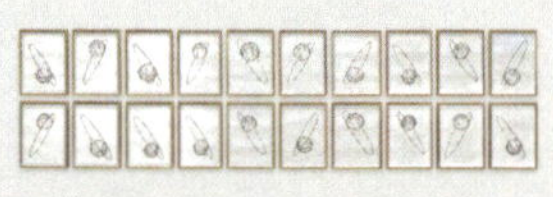

Royden Rabinowitch (*1943)
Judgments on Conformal Transformations, May 1996
set of 20 drawings, pastel on paper
29.7 × 21 cm
(each piece unframed)
MAMCO collection
gift of Christian Bernard
inv.: 1996–491 (1 to 20)

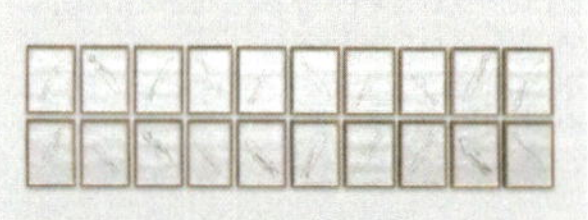

Royden Rabinowitch (*1943)
Judgments on Conformal Transformations, April 1996
set of 20 drawings, pastel on paper
29.7 × 21 cm
(each piece unframed)
MAMCO collection
gift of Christian Bernard
inv.: 1996–490 (1 to 20)

Alessandro Gallicchio teaches art history at Sorbonne Université. He owns a PHD from the Università degli studi di Firenze, the Universität Bonn, and Sorbonne Université. His most recent researches led to the creation of *MonuMed* (Monumentalisation et espace urbain dans les Balkans et en Méditerranée), a project devoted to art and human sciences, and to the publication of *Monument en mouvements. Artistes et chercheurs face à la monumentalisation contemporaine* (Gli Ori, 2020). In 2020, he got the André Chastel grant from the Villa Médicis (Rome) for a project studying urban traces of Mediterranean colonial empires. He explored this topic in the show *Rue d'Alger* on the occasion of Manifesta 13 Marseille. In 2021, he was in residence at the Ecole française of Athens.

Sophie Costes is an art historian. Since 1995, she's curator in charge of the collection at MAMCO. She also writes since 2015 for SIKART, a biographical dictionary on art in Switzerland.

Imprint

Editorial Direction
Lionel Bovier

Editorial Coordination and Redaction
Thierry Davila

Translation
Nicholas Huckle

Proofreading
Thierry Davila
Ambroise Tièche

Texts
Sophie Costes
Alessandro Gallicchio

Design
Gavillet & Cie/Devaud

Typefaces
Apax, Practice (www.optimo.ch)

Published with ARTBOOKID.A.P.
75 Brood Street, Suite 630, New York
NY 10004, www.artbook.com

ISBN 9781636810430

Production
Musumeci S.p.A.
Quart (Aosta)
Italy

Printed and bound in Europe

Photos Credits
→ Ilmari Kalkkinen
pp. 2–9
→ Annik Wetter
for the other images

Acknowledgments
Franck Maes, Chantal Kleinmeulman.
We thank Royden Rabinowitch for his help, confidence, and involvement in this project and Saba Flesch for her precious help.

The series "MAMCO Collection" is realized thanks to the support of the Leenaards Foundation

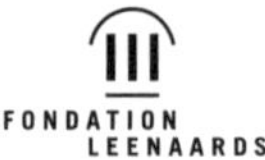

MAMCO
GENEVE

10 rue des Vieux-Grenadiers
CH–1205 Geneva
T +41 22 320 61 22
F + 41 22 781 56 81
E info@mamco.ch

MAMCO opened in 1994 thanks to the perseverance of AMAM (Association for a Modern Art Museum, now Friends of MAMCO) and the generosity of eight patrons, who created the FONDATION MAMCO. Pooling together the support of its Founders and, later, its Co-founders, the foundation was the main source of funding and the sole governing body of the museum up until 2005, when it joined forces with the State and City of Geneva to create a public foundation, known as FONDAMCO.

MAMCO is overseen by FONDAMCO, which is made up of FONDATION MAMCO, the Canton, and City of Geneva. FONDAMCO would like to thank all its partners, both public and private, and in particular: JTI, Fondation Leenaards, and Fondation Valeria Rossi di Montelera, as well as Fondation de bienfaisance du Groupe Pictet, Fondation Bru, Fondation Coromandel, Fondation Lombard Odier, Lenz & Stählin, Mirabaud & Cie SA, Christie's, and Sotheby's.

FONDAMCO

Philippe Bertherat, President
Ronald Asmar, Vice President
Carine Bachmann
Michèle Freiburghaus-Lens
Patrick Fuchs
Jean-Pierre Greff
Jérôme Massard
Marc-André Renold
Simon Studer

FONDATION MAMCO

Council
Philippe Bertherat, President
Pierre de Labouchere, Vice President
Jean Marc Annicchiarico, Treasurer
Karma Liess-Shakarchi, Secretary
Charle Beer
Simon Studer

Founders
Claude Barbey
Jean-Paul Croisier
Pierre Darier
André L'Huillier
Philippe Nordmann
Pierre Mirabaud
Bernard Sabrier
—as well as the Friends Association, represented by its President, Patrick Fuchs

Co-founders
Anne-Shelton et Jean-Michel Aaron
Tonie and Philippe Bertherat
Marc Blondeau
Maryse Bory
Nicole Ghez de Castelnuovo
Bénédict Hentsch
Christina and Pierre de Labouchere
Aimery Langlois-Meurinne
Jean-Léonard de Meuron
Nadine and Edmond de Rothschild
Lily and Edmond Safra

Patrons
Afshan Almassi Sturzda
Jean Marc Annicchiarico
Tonie and Philippe Bertherat
Verena and Rémy Best
Marc Blondeau
Maryse Bory
Jean-Paul Croisier
Darier Family
Zaza and Philippe Jabre
Christina and Pierre de Labouchere
Karma Liess-Shakarchi
Emmanuelle Maillard
Jean-Léonard de Meuron
Patricia and Jean-Pierre Michaux
Pierre Mirabaud
Jacqueline and Philippe Nordmann
Alain-Dominique Perrin
Marine and Claude Robert
Bernard Sabrier
Lily Safra, represented by Samuel Elia
Simon Studer

TEAM

Lionel Bovier, Director

Museum Management and Development
Nicole Boissonnas, Public Relations and Development
Chloë Gouédard, Library, Archives, and Museum Ressources
Julien Gremaud, Digital Communication
Viviane Reybier, Press and Communication

Exhibitions and Collection
Julien Fronsacq, Chief Curator
Françoise Ninghetto, Honorary Curator
Sophie Costes, Collection Curator
Paul Bernard, Curator
Fabrice Stroun, Associate Curator
Cyrille Maillot, Chief Exhibition Productions
Filipe Dos Santos, Exhibition Productions and Collection Registrar
Pierre-Antoine Héritier and Caroline Dick, Associate Restorers
Annik Wetter, Associate Photographer

Public and Education Services
Yann Abrecht, Public Services Manager
Mathilde Acevedo, Public Services Coordinator
Daniel Maury, Public Services Coordinator
Charlotte Morel, Education Services Manager
Julie Cudet, Education Services Coordinator
Thierry Davila, Curator in Charge of Publications

Facility Management and Surveillance
Antonio Magalhes, Chief of Facility Management
Maria de Fatima Braganca, Facility Management
Joana Gomes Da Silva, Facility Management
Carlos Martins Fonseca, Surveillance
Luc Schuwey, Surveillance

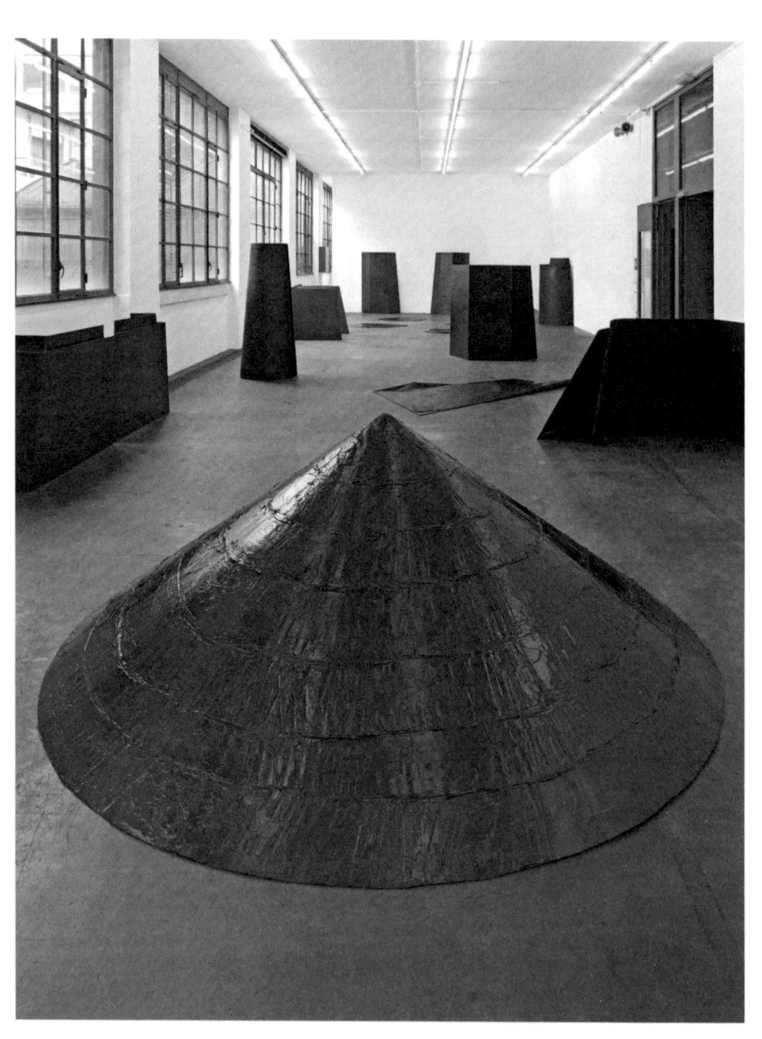